Better Homes and Gardens®

step-by-step

annuals

Peter Loewer

Better Homes and Gardens® Books
Des Moines, Iowa

Better Homes and Gardens® Books
An imprint of Meredith® Books

Step-by-Step Annuals
Senior Editor: Marsha Jahns
Production Manager: Douglas Johnston

Vice President and Editorial Director: Elizabeth P. Rice
Executive Editor: Kay Sanders
Art Director: Ernest Shelton
Managing Editor: Christopher Cavanaugh

President, Book Group: Joseph J. Ward
Vice President, Retail Marketing: Jamie L. Martin
Vice President, Direct Marketing: Timothy Jarrell

Meredith Corporation
Chairman of the Executive Committee: E. T. Meredith III
Chairman of the Board and Chief Executive Officer:
   Jack D. Rehm
President and Chief Operating Officer: William T. Kerr

Produced by ROUNDTABLE PRESS, INC.
Directors: Susan E. Meyer, Marsha Melnick
Executive Editor: Amy T. Jonak
Editorial Director: Anne Halpin
Senior Editor: Jane Mintzer Hoffman
Design: Brian Sisco, Susan Evans, Sisco & Evans, New York
Photo Editor: Marisa Bulzone
Assistant Photo Editor: Carol Sattler
Encyclopedia Editor: Henry W. Art and Storey
   Communications, Inc., Pownal, Vermont
Horticultural Consultant: Christine M. Douglas
Copy Editors: Paula Bakule, Sue Heinemann, Amy K. Hughes
Proofreader: Cathy Peck
Editorial Assistant: Alexis Wilson
Step-by-Step Photography: Derek Fell
Garden Plans: Elayne Sears and Storey Communications, Inc.

All of us at Meredith® Books are dedicated to providing you
with the information and ideas you need for successful gardening. We guarantee your satisfaction with this book for as long
as you own it. If you have any questions, comments, or suggestions, please write to us at:

Meredith® Books, *Garden Books*
Editorial Department, RW206
1716 Locust St.
Des Moines, IA 50309–3023

STEP-BY-STEP

Annuals

The Annual Garden

*W*hat exactly are garden annuals? Botanically, they are plants that germinate, mature, flower, and produce seed in one year. • Many gardeners also include in the grouping a few biennials (plants that take two years to go from germinating to producing seed)—ones that will blossom the first year when conditions are correct. We can also count as annuals a number of perennials that bloom in their first year, plus hundreds of plants from warm parts of the world that bloom in their first year but perish when temperatures plummet, unless sheltered in a warm place during the cold winter months. • Then, too, there are dozens of bulbous plants, such as dahlias or caladiums, that are used for one season and then tossed out or dug up and stored indoors over winter. • This book includes all these kinds of plants.

Improved Favorites

Unfortunately, when most gardeners think of annuals they picture the old warhorses: petunias, marigolds, and zinnias. But even these flowers have a new look for today. For example, plant breeders have produced new cultivars of zinnias in appealing colors that now include many pastels in addition to the primary colors of old. Flowers have become larger, and many blossoms now have double the original number of petals. Today heights vary from very short plants to some that are 3 feet tall, and most have an expanded flowering season. One zinnia cultivar, 'Peter Pan', is a foot-high hedge with 3-inch white, pink, orange, and gold flowers.

Annuals boast amazing flowers and often offer vibrant foliage. Not only do they add delightful color to a border, but they are also wonderful as cut flowers. And many annuals bloom quickly, some in less than eight weeks from the time seed is planted. If spent flowers are removed regularly, annuals continue to bloom until the summer's end, in contrast to perennials, which flower for just a few weeks to a month before retreating until the next garden season.

Annuals are easy to grow, too. Because most must bloom in one garden season, their soil requirements are usually not as demanding as those of most perennials. You may well have seen marigolds continue to bloom and bloom even though they've been planted in a hot, dry place and neglected for weeks on end.

In the long run, annuals require less care than perennials, which must be clipped, trimmed, fed, and in colder climates, often mulched for the winter in order to survive for a second season. What's more, you must periodically divide mature perennials or they will hold back on flowering.

An annual garden is easy to design, requiring less planning than a perennial garden, where you must take care to provide future space for plants to expand.

Annuals give the gardener a chance to really experiment with color and texture combinations. If your plan for one year doesn't work, you can make a whole new plan for the next year.

Annuals are very effective when mixed with perennials—including shrubs and even trees. They can fill the empty spaces in the garden until the slower plants grow and mature.

Finally, annuals, especially when you grow them from seed, are very inexpensive; even when purchased at a garden center, they are always cheaper than perennials. And annuals easily adapt to pot and container culture. They can withstand temperature fluctuations, and they usually recover if you forget to water them.

▼ Kinds of Annuals

Although some gardeners buy their annuals at garden centers, the majority start their plants from seed purchased by mail from the catalogues of seed houses.

Seeds for annual plants are usually available as *standards,* where pollination has occurred naturally in the field, or as *hybrids,* which are produced by controlling pollination between selected parents (many times by hand). The first-generation results of these deliberate crossings are called F1 hybrids; they are more expensive than ordinary seed selections because of the manual labor needed to produce them. The best of these hybrids take characteristics from both parents, and many are very spectacular plants. Unfortunately, due to the laws of heredity, F1 hybrids frequently do not breed true and must continue to be propagated at the nursery. This means that seed saved from F1 hybrids will usually yield only disappointment to the gardener.

English gardeners devised the first system for describing habits of seed germination for annuals. They divided annual plants into three categories: hardy, half-hardy, and tender.

Hardy annuals are those that tolerate a reasonable degree of frost and freezing. Even in the northern United States and parts of Canada, their seeds will survive a winter outside and germinate in the spring.

Half-hardy annuals are damaged, set back, or killed by repeated exposure to frost, but most will withstand an occasional light frost and revel in endless days of cool, even wet weather, which is common in the Northwest.

Unusual Annuals

There are hundreds of unusual annuals available from nurseries and mail-order seed catalogues.The tassel flower (Emilia javanica) bears many red flowers that look like small paintbrushes or Victorian curtain tassels. Most morning-glories climb, but there is one annual species, the bush morning-glory (Convolvulus tricolor) that grows about 1 foot tall, then becomes a ground cover with variegated leaves and blue, pink, or purple flowers of great charm. Or try the lovely wishbone flower (Torenia fournieri), with 1-foot plants that bear lovely violet-blue flowers and two stamens that look like a wishbone.

Woolflower (Celosia cristata) has some of the most unusually shaped flowers in the plant world. Some of the flower heads are fluffy plumes or spires, but others are twisted into shapes resembling undersea coral or roosters' combs. A bed of these interesting flowers, with their often brilliant colors, creates a bold statement.

The lacy yellow-green seed heads and ferny leaves of dill, most often seen in herb gardens, make an unusual and quite lovely partner for bright pink cosmos daisies.

Tender annuals come from warm parts of the world. They need warm soil for germination to occur and are immediately killed by frost.

▼ About Botanical Names

Many plants have common names like dahlias or dandelions, and when we hear that name everyone pictures the same flower. But how about tassel flower? There are at least two plants known as tassel flower, and they look quite different. One tassel flower—the one also known as love-lies-bleeding—is a large-leaved plant with long, drooping clusters of minute pink or red flowers that look like chenille. The other tassel flower (also called Flora's-paintbrush) bears double daisylike flowers in red or bright yellow.

To avoid confusion a system of botanical names was devised, and Latin was used because it's the universal language of science. The first tassel flower described above is classified as *Amaranthus caudatus,* the second one is *Emilia javanica.* Don't be worried about saying a Latin name aloud. Very few gardeners can pronounce all these names correctly. As long as you are close, most people will know what you mean.

Four terms are in general use for botanical names of particular plants: genus, species, variety, and cultivar. The genus name designates a group of plants that are closely related, and the species name suggests an individual plant's unique quality, like flower color or stature. Imagine three brothers with the last name of Smith who all have a family resemblance. But Tom is tall and Jim has blond hair and George has green eyes. We might say that the genus is Smith and one species is, for example, Tom. In print, the genus name is capitalized and italicized, and the species is in lowercase italics.

Then there is the word "variety." A plant variety is one that develops a noticeable change in character that remains true from generation to generation, such as a large red flower in a species of small yellow flowers. Varieties develop in the wild, as spontaneous mutations.

Finally there is "cultivar," a term introduced in 1923 by L. H. Bailey as a shorthand for *culti*vated *vari*ety. It is distinguished in print by being set inside single quotation marks. A cultivar is a plant variety that appears in cultivation and could occur either by chance or design. It is not necessary for a cultivar to breed true from seed, but many do. Most gardeners and nursery catalogues interchange the terms "variety" and "cultivar" continually.

Taking cosmos daisies as an example, the genus name is *Cosmos*, the species is *bipinnatus*, and when the flower petals are curved in on themselves like delicate shells, the cultivar is 'Sea Shells'.

The gardener should be reminded that many flowers listed in today's catalogues have botanical names that are woefully out of date. This is because catalogue copywriters realize that the gardening public often becomes attached to a particular name and it takes generations to change their minds.

But names will never change the beauty of the flowers that we call annuals. Use this book to discover how these wonderful flowers can add beauty to your home garden.

CHAPTER 1

Designing Your Garden

*a*nnuals easily delight the eye with their colorful flowers. To take full advantage of the allure of annuals, you should first prepare a plan for your garden. • You can plant annuals in a formal or informal design by themselves, combined with perennials, or as fillers between shrubs. Take care to select the best plants for the specific conditions of your site. Consider not only how the flower colors will mix and match, but also the effect of different heights, textures, shapes, sizes, and fragrances. • This chapter offers tips to get you started, but the final selection is a personal one. With hundreds of annuals to choose from it's easy to find a number of combinations that you like.

Making a Plan

*B*efore you plant the first seed, take a pencil or pen and a piece of paper and draw a simple plan for the garden. Design the garden around existing features on your property. Make sure, for example, that your garden will not block the path that connects the garage with the kitchen door or the walkway between a child's play area and the back porch.

Also think about the people who will use the garden. If elderly or disabled people spend time in the garden, avoid steep pathways or slippery surfaces. Be sure to consider where children and pets may romp in the garden. And don't forget to evaluate the needs of the person who mows the lawn.

When making your plan, look for vacant spaces between existing shrubs or perennial flowers—you can use annuals to fill in these spots. Annuals also make great edging plants for paths and walkways.

Be sure to put existing trees on your plan, as few if any annuals, aside from impatiens and caladiums, will do well in the shade of most lawn trees.

You'll also want to consider the size of a lawn. Large lawns around small houses are generally out of scale, but a small lawn or grass pathway around or into a garden can act as a frame to a fine piece of property and glorify the flowering plants.

Then, too, nothing beats a cutting garden, a place where annuals are planted not for an aesthetic design but simply to serve as a continual source of flowers for decorating the house and the dinner table.

Always consider the sun's path when planning a garden, and the availability of water, especially if your summers are hot and dry. Most annuals like sun, and if you put the garden in a heavily shaded area, the choice of annuals diminishes. In northern gardens

The deep green foliage and dark shadows of a woodland offer a perfect backdrop for the bright flowers of sun-loving annuals and perennials growing in an open, sunny garden.

Terraced beds of annuals border the steps and path leading down the slope from a house.

Sun-loving nicotiana stars in this informal meadowy garden in the country.

Making a Plan CONTINUED

only a little shade is ever advisable, but in the Deep South and the Southwest, a bit of afternoon shade can be beneficial to most annuals.

And don't forget the weather. If storms in your region come in from the east, try to place the garden where it will have some small measure of protection, especially during summer.

Pay some attention to the soil. If you have nothing but solid clay and little time or money to make or buy compost and other materials to modify the soil, then a garden of raised beds (edged with railroad ties or stone) would be best.

Allow room in the garden for the gardener, with narrow pathways or stepping stones. Without such niceties, weeding and general garden maintenance will

A carefully planned garden of the most common annuals can mimic the sophisticated look of a grand perennial border. Group plants in flowing drifts, and gradually increase the heights of plants from the front to the back of the garden.

The strict formality of a precisely edged square bed is enlivened by an exuberant color scheme pairing brilliant red cannas and zinnias with purple heart (Setcreasea pallida) *and the fluffy plumes of an annual fountain grass* (Pennisetum setaceum).

Cheerful California poppies (Eschscholzia californica) spill over the edge of a stone wall and soften the look of the masonry. Their bright colors stand up to the strongest sunlight.

always be difficult and awkward. Gardens are for enjoyment, and maintaining them should be a pleasure, not a dreaded chore.

Lastly, be true to the site. Bringing in tons of stone to make a mountain in the middle of flat country or trying to create a desert garden where it rains five days a week will lead to hours of extra work, endless frustration, and few good times in the garden.

Once you have decided on a garden site, it's important to consider how you will get there, especially when you are loaded up with tools. A pathway to the garden can be as simple as a layer of pine needles or pine bark set between plastic, metal, or wooden edging. Or it can be paved with crushed stone, or even made of fieldstones with grass in between. Whatever kind of pathway you decide to make, it should be able to withstand the weight of a wheelbarrow full of garden tools or a lot of foot traffic. And a good path will help keep dirt and grass clippings from being tracked back into the house.

Annuals massed in neatly shaped beds separated by strips of manicured lawn create a formal look. Blue-violet and white salvia and other bedding plants are kept under strict control.

Formal and Informal Garden Shapes

Carpet Beds

Victorian-style carpet beds created the look of Oriental rugs using bedding annuals instead of wool. They were very popular floral and foliage displays in parks and grand lawns and are still popular today.

Annuals suited for such displays include Irish lace (Tagetes filifolia), sweet alyssum (Lobularia maritima), flossflower (Ageratum spp.), coleus (Coleus spp.), bedding or wax begonia (B. × semperflorens-cultorum), celosia (C. cristata), ornamental pepper (Capsicum annuum), dusty-miller (Centaurea and Senecio spp.), polka-dot plant (Hypoestes phyllostachya), perilla (P. frutescens), bloodleaf plant (Iresine herbstii), and various geraniums (Pelargonium spp.).

Use just about any plant that blooms all summer (deadheading is mandatory in this type of garden), responds to clipping, and grows reasonably low to the ground.

Gardens come in many shapes, ranging from formal squares and rectangles to clear-cut circles and ovals, to free-form areas called island beds, which can be loosely circular or oval, or kidney-shaped like coffee tables from the 1950s.

A garden with a formal shape, especially one with straight edges and right-angled corners, looks best in a clearly defined area. Use such a garden to complement a house with a formal design, or tuck it in a small space between the front of a townhouse and the sidewalk or curb.

Very large square beds look fine in front of large brick Colonial houses, but they appear out of place in front of small Cape Cod homes. With this style of home a less-defined garden in an informal shape is more appropriate.

1 *Create an instant carpet bed with plants. Mark the pattern on the ground with lime or string. Set plants in their containers into the prepared bed to check the pattern.*

Annuals massed in a geometric mandala pattern update the colorful carpet beds of Victorian gardens. Common plants create the look here: yellow and orange marigolds, a lavender sweet alyssum cultivar, and a deep violet variety of edging lobelia.

2 *Start at one end and plant across the bed, or fill areas of the same color one at a time. Leave enough space between small plants to allow them to grow to full size.*

3 *After planting is complete, water well. This contrasting combination of red-violet and yellow-green* Alternanthera *needs less maintenance than a bed of flowers.*

Cottage Gardens

Cottage gardens are front yards full of exuberant flowers, including vines, sunflowers, herbs, and even some vegetables for the table.

Ideally a cottage garden design should feature a prominent pathway to the front door and an outside border of permanent shrubbery with everything else growing in a seemingly wild profusion of color. You might include pansies (Viola × wittrockiana), annual phlox (Phlox drummondii), pinks (Dianthus spp.), spider flowers (Cleome hasslerana), sunflowers (Helianthus annuus), all sorts of zinnias and marigolds, and any other annuals you can squeeze in.

Although it's meant to look rustic, a cottage garden is labor-intensive. Once a plant dies or goes out of bloom, it must be quickly replaced. Only plant what you can care for.

If the garden is next to acres of wide open field, a formal look should be tempered with some acknowledgment of the wild spaces nearby. Allow for a gradual visual transition from garden to field by softening the garden's edge and eliminating sharp lines. It also helps to increase the size of the plants gradually as they come close to the field, perhaps by planting some castor beans *(Ricinus communis)* or ornamental grasses at the back of the garden.

Where large stretches of lawn are available, what's known as an English island bed may be the best approach. Here the garden becomes an island surrounded by a sea of grass. The island's shape can be simple or complex, but bear in mind that simpler garden shapes are much easier to maintain than complicated outlines.

A long, narrow lot is often very difficult to work with. Here, two small, fairly formal gardens may be most effective. Or, if you have both time and energy, a large, informal garden may be feasible, especially if you construct pathways that wind between the flower beds and leave a spot in the center of the garden where you can just sit and look out upon the flowers.

With some creativity, you'll discover there are as many shapes for gardens as there are plants to grow.

Designing with Plants

Tall Plants

Most annuals grow as mounds of plants dotted with flowers. To bring an element of surprise to a staid arrangement, try interweaving low plants with tall, spiky annuals. Winged everlastings (Ammobium alatum) have 3-foot-high stems topped with small white everlasting flowers. Giant cultivars of cannas produce 7-foot columns of upright foliage topped with glorious flaming-bright flowers. The really brilliant feathered blossoms of the crested types of celosia exhibit sharp-pointed 1-foot plumes on top of 2-foot plants. Tall-growing salvias can reach 4 feet high and are dazzlingly colored.

When gardening with annuals there are more plant characteristics to consider than the color of flowers. Take height, for example. Some plants, like flossflowers *(Ageratum houstonianum)*, are short; others, like spider flowers *(Cleome hasslerana)*, can reach 4 or 5 feet, and sunflowers *(Helianthus annuus)* can tower over the tallest gardener.

Plant height is an important design factor. Traditional rules say put taller plants at the back and shorter plants in the front of the garden, but the rules can be broken. Sometimes a taller plant surrounded by smaller flowers acts like a living sculpture. Or try planting some morning-glories *(Ipomoea tricolor)* so that their blossoming vines can climb the stems of a tall spider flower.

Consider flower texture too. When in bloom, the annual cloud grass *(Agrostis nebulosa)* looks like a low cloud or ground fog from even a short distance. Woolflowers *(Celosia cristata)* look decidedly artificial, resembling feathers or pieces of coral, and their blossoms actually glisten in sunlight. Love-lies-bleeding *(Amaranthus caudatus)* bears long, drooping wands of tiny flowers that look like chenille.

The needlelike leaves of summer cypress *(Kochia scoparia)* make this plant look more like a dwarf conifer than an annual. Castor beans *(Ricinus communis)* have broad tropical-like foliage, and the 6-foot-high plants can add a jungle touch to even a northern garden. The colorful, frilly heads of ornamental kale *(Brassica oleracea)* look more like bridal bouquets than vegetables.

For pure color, coleus leaves are as brightly colored as any piece of fabric you can buy, while the flowers of the Bonfire salvia *(S. splendens* 'Bonfire') are so red they can overpower all other nearby flowers.

When designing with plants, all the visual qualities are important, from flower to leaf to size to texture. And mixing them all together makes creating a garden like working on a canvas, using a brush loaded with living plants instead of paint.

Cassia 'California Gold' bears bright yellow blossoms on bushy plants that add mass as well as color to a bed or border.

Towering spider flower (Cleome hasslerana) *is an ideal plant for the back of annual beds and borders.*

A neat row of silvery white dusty-miller (Senecio cineraria) makes a classic edging for a sunny garden of mealy-cup sage (Salvia farinacea 'Victoria'), spider flowers (Cleome hasslerana), and other annuals.

For a lush look, mass plants of different heights. This lively border combines tall cosmos in rosy red, pink, and white; yellow marigolds of intermediate height; and a low edging of dusty-miller.

Annuals as Edgings

Lavish plantings of colorful zinnias, cosmos, spider flowers, and other annuals edge a small lawn and make an urban property look and feel considerably larger than it really is.

*A*lmost everything looks better when framed, whether it's a painting, a tapestry, or a garden. When edging garden pathways many gardeners simply choose low-growing and clump-forming plants and set them along the garden's borders. Edgings of wax begonias, lobelias, sweet alyssum, verbenas (*Verbena × hybrida*—especially the cultivar 'Peaches and Cream'), or low-growing petunias, pansies, or even Livingstone daisies *(Dorotheanthus bellidiformis)* become delightful boundaries between the garden proper and the lawn or a pathway.

Excellent borders can also be made by using plants as clumps of color, each clump to be met by a collection of new plants.

For sunny borders, dahlias are easy to grow from seed and will bloom by early summer if started indoors four to six weeks before the last frost in your area (at the end of the season the tuberous roots can be dug up and stored over the winter in a cool spot). Dahlia cultivars, such as the low-growing 'Piccolo Mixed', consist of flowers ranging from white to yellow to pink to orange. Mass these blooms at the border's edge.

If your garden gets light shade, try short caladiums, such as the cultivar 'Little Miss Muffet', compact plants about 8 inches tall with lime green leaves spashed with dots of red. Plant these caladiums in a clump, then let them fade away to a double line of lobelias or some of the dwarf bedding carnations or the Fairway Series of dwarf coleus with colors of red velvet, bronze, yellow, or rose. Only 8 to 10 inches high, these coleus are especially fine in a partly shaded area.

And no edging plants beat China pinks *(Dianthus chinensis)*, with their fringed petals and scarlet centers fading to pink.

1 An edging of low-growing annuals softens the sharp line of a path or wall, to give the garden a finished look. With a hoe or cultivator, loosen the soil before planting.

2 Set plants along the front of the garden, spacing them the correct distance apart (see the Encyclopedia beginning on page 96 for spacing information). Water well.

3 A few weeks later the plants will have filled in the empty space. Wishbone flower (Torenia fournieri), shown here, makes a charming edging for shady beds and borders.

Edging Plants

The following annuals are excellent when used to edge a garden: Swan River daisy (Brachycome *spp.*); *creeping zinnia* (Sanvitalia *'Mandarin Orange'*), *an annual that bears 1-inch-wide flowers above creeping stems never more than 6 inches high; and French marigolds* (Tagetes patula), *small plants with cultivars of many colors including 'Sophia', the Hero Series, and the Zenith Series. Or choose the 8-inch-high annual phlox covered with starlike blossoms. Love-in-a-mist* (Nigella damascena) *produces attractive flowers and fernlike foliage and has seedpods that look like jester's caps. And there are flossflowers, low-growing nicotianas, pansies, and cultivars of the zinnia, Z. angustifolia 'Golden Orange' and 'Alba'. For shady areas use impatiens or the beautiful polka-dot plant* (Hypoestes phyllostachya).

Annual Vines

Vines can literally cover a multitude of sins. They will twine around an unwanted stump or crawl around that pile of garden debris that never seems to get cleared away. Vines can turn an ugly concrete wall into something out of an English cottage garden, and an offensive fence becomes a lovely garden backdrop when you let a vine ramble up and over its boundaries. Japanese hops *(Humulus japonicus)* will often grow 30 feet high in a good year and may not only cover an unwanted heap of rubbish but begin to cover the garage as well.

Not all vines are so voracious and greedy. Many of the morning-glories amble along, producing their lovely flowers. In addition to beautiful scarlet-orange flowers, the scarlet runner bean *(Phaseolus coccineus)* bears edible pods. You can grow these vines to shade a front porch by letting them climb strings stretched from the porch rail to the edge of the roof above.

Instead of awnings or shutters, try screening a window with a vine to shade the room from summer's brightness. Most garden stores now stock various

Hyacinth bean (Dolichos lablab) *covers the arch above a garden gate with clusters of purple flowers that are followed with edible beans.*

Scarlet runner beans make a decorative screen or background when trained on lattice, a trellis, or an arbor, and they offer the bonus of edible beans.

The huge, trumpet-shaped flowers of angel's trumpet (Brugmansia) *lend a tropical touch to the garden. But be careful because the plant is poisonous.*

Canary creeper (Tropaeolum peregrinum) *is a vining cousin of the nasturtium, with fringed canary yellow blossoms that look like small birds perched among the lobed leaves.*

Nasturtiums (Tropaeolum majus) *are vining plants that can be trained as climbers. In this garden their bright blossoms intertwine with a climbing rose, 'Golden Showers.'*

Black-Eyed Susan Vine

The black-eyed Susan vine (Thunbergia alata) *is a tender perennial grown as an annual because it flowers the first year from seed. Unlike many annual vines, this is not an excessive or rampant grower and will usually stay 6 to 8 feet long or less. The light green arrow-shaped leaves are set off by 1½-inch-wide yellow, cream, or orange flowers with dark purple to black centers. Thunbergias look lovely spilling over the edge of a hanging basket. Plants can be set at the edge of a wall so that the stems will twine down between the stones or, if left without supports, they will trail along the ground. In areas with warm winters where the ground does not really freeze, the vines will overwinter.*

ready-made trellises of wood (usually in 4- by 8-foot sections) or sturdy white plastic, which actually fold for storage. You can even make a trellis of brass cup hooks strung with fishing line or heavy twine.

One of the most wonderful vines is the moonflower *(Ipomoea alba),* a tropical perennial grown as an annual in the North. This vine will reach 10 feet in a warm summer but never becomes a threat because it can easily be pruned. The pure white flowers, with a sweet scent of cinnamon and vanilla, are 6 inches wide on a 6-inch tube. As evening descends, the flowers slowly open, only to fade away with the first flush of dawn. Plant them around a lantern post and you will have flowers to brighten every summer evening.

Cardinal climber *(Ipomoea × multifida)* is an annual twiner with deeply cut arrow-shaped leaves and bright red flowers. Cypress vine *(I. quamoclit)* has finely cut leaves that look like feathers, and beautiful scarlet flowers that range along the stems as they crawl through the garden. Try growing them with yellow dahlias. In areas with light winters, the seed will survive from year to year.

Finally, don't overlook the lablab, or hyacinth bean *(Dolichos lablab).* This perennial vine blooms like an annual, with lovely purple pealike flowers, followed by 6-inch pods that resemble the sounding board of a beautiful antique cello.

Foliage Plants

TIMESAVING TIP

Grow a double-duty foliage plant in your annual garden this year. For example, Purple Ruffles basil (Ocimum basilicum 'Purple Ruffles') has frilly leaves of deep bronzy purple that look stunning with pink or pale yellow flowers, and offer their marvelous flavor for kitchen use.

*A*nnuals provide more than flowers in the garden; they have interesting foliage, too. The brightest patch of color you see in a garden of annuals, especially a shady garden, could well come from the leaves of coleus, not from flowers. The hybrid *Coleus* 'Rainbow Mix' has leaves that are red, orange, rose, pink, chartreuse, copper, purple streaked with red, ivory ringed with green, or bright gold dashed here and there with green flecks. From a few dollars' worth of seeds, you can be blessed with dozens of plants in a wide array of colors.

There are many annuals that have wonderful foliage but those listed and shown here and on page 25 are widely available. The foliage of perilla *(P. frutescens)*, for example, has the texture of seersucker and a reddish purple color streaked with metallic overtones. Purple Ruffles basil *(Ocimum basilicum 'Purple Ruffles')* has purple-black foliage with serrated leaves that look as though they'd been cut with pinking shears. And nothing is more startlingly attractive than a temporary hedge of summer cypress *(Kochia scoparia* var. *tricophylla)*, especially the cultivar 'Acapulco Silver', whose light green leaves are dusted with silver. Polka-dot plants *(Hypoestes phyllostachya)* are marvelous planted in a group, surrounded by blooming annuals including wishbone flowers *(Torenia fournieri)* or dark pink impatiens.

Plant foliage annuals around the garden to highlight any temporarily dull section. By growing or buying foliage annuals in pots, you can design a garden using only foliage color and texture. If a combination doesn't suit you, simply move the pot around until the design is set.

Summer cypress (Kochia scoparia 'Acapulco Silver') looks like a shrub, but it's an annual. At the end of the season the foliage turns brilliant red.

Coleus foliage brings color and texture to annual gardens. Garden centers usually offer a few varieties, but many more are available in seed form.

Extravagant Foliage

Some annual plants with striking foliage are Jacob's-coat (Acalypha wilkesiana), garden orach (Atriplex hortensis), red Malabar spinach (Basella alba 'Rubra'), ornamental kale (Brassica oleracea), caladium (C. × hortulanum), dwarf canna (C. × generalis), dusty-miller (Centaurea cineraria or Chrysanthemum ptarmiciflorum 'Silver Feather'), elephant's-ear (Colocasia esculenta), bush morning-glory (Convolvulus tricolor), snow-on-the-mountain (Euphorbia marginata), fennel (Foeniculum vulgare), red hedging hibiscus (H. acetosella 'Red Shield'), hops (Humulus japonicus), blood-leaf (Iresine herbstii), curled mallow (Malva verticillata var. crispa), fountain grass (Pennisetum setaceum), Irish lace (Tagetes filifolia), dwarf nasturtium (Tropaeolum minus 'Alaska Mixed'), and canary creeper (Tropaeolum peregrinum).

Flowering maple (Abutilon hybridum) can be grown as a houseplant or an outdoor annual. This cultivar has variegated leaves that are splashed with yellow.

Caladiums grow from tender bulbs that are treated as annuals in all but the warmest climates. The large, colorful leaves bring a touch of the tropics to shady gardens.

Working with Color

Color and Space

A small garden can be made to look much larger by clever use of color, in line with the phenomenon of atmospheric perspective, by which colors look paler as they recede into the distance.

To create the illusion of perspective in the garden, choose different cultivars of the same species of plant, with flower color ranging from bright to medium to pale, even white. Start at the front end of the border with the darkest color. Set lighter-colored plants behind it; then use even lighter colors. When viewed together, the colors look as though they were fading into the distance.

The same effect can be achieved by using various cultivars of caladiums, starting with bright red, fading to rose, then pink, and finally white.

Whether you choose annuals with bright flowers, bright foliage, or both, you need to consider how different colors interact in the garden.

It's amazing just how many color combinations work in the garden. You'll soon see that working with color in the landscape is not all that difficult. Books have been written about using color when arranging plants and flowers—especially in English borders—but you don't need so much knowledge and effort for success.

Remember that garden design is the owner's personal statement and one gardener's love of bright colors might be despised by the person next door, who believes that the only successful flower groupings combine maroon and olive green. There are no hard-and-fast rules for color combination.

Most important to consider is the brightness or intensity of the flower or foliage color. In a mixed border of bright orange and yellow marigolds and cosmos daisies, a few pale pink verbenas stuck here and there would be almost invisible. The same holds true for putting five flaming red geraniums in the center of a 6-foot oval of yellow marigolds—unless you are trying to approximate a dragon's eye, this design probably won't succeed as a flower bed.

In general, try combining deep blues with clear, soft yellows and use pale blues with pale pinks. When using deep purples, try paler tints of the same color, or ivory white, or pale yellow. Pure orange works well with bronze and brown, and yellow harmonizes well with soft blues and creamy whites. And all the oranges work well together.

White, silver, and gray, whether from flower or foliage, lead to a quiet, contemplative look, and a garden built on these tones appears much larger than it really is.

A harmonious color scheme of purples and pinks, brightened with touches of white, is achieved with blue-violet Victoria salvia (rear), deep purple heliotrope, pink powder-puff zinnias, and pink and white nicotiana (foreground).

If you opt for a predominantly single-color garden, you can add interest to the design by including some white flowers for freshness and sparkle. This romantic corner garden combines red Flanders poppies (Papaver rhoeas) with white nicotiana, which gives off a sweet scent at night.

Violas in complementary colors of purple and yellow bloom in the cool weather of a northern spring, or in the winter in warm climates.

An elegant all-white garden looks cool and refreshing on a hot day. This one contains tall spider flowers and cosmos, nicotiana, and white edging lobelia with a few purple plants interspersed.

Working with Color CONTINUED

In addition to color, think about size. A few short pink bedding begonias would be overpowered by a bunch of 4- to 6-foot-high sunflowers. And any discussion of size quickly turns to the concept of massing flowers and foliage. Many annual flowers look best when displayed in the company of others of their kind. For example, orange-red tassel flowers *(Emilia javanica)* are charming, but the bright color of their small blooms makes more of an impact when dozens of plants are seeded in one spot. While the foliage of any of the dusty-millers is attractive enough in small amounts, the plants really make a statement when several of them are put together in the bed or border.

And don't forget the garden in the evening. As the sky darkens, blues and purples deepen and become less obvious, but white and light yellow flowers retain their brightness. Instead of being washed out as the light begins to fade, white flowers can be beacons of light here and there in the gloom.

Cool blues and purples mix well with pinks. Above, left to right, are rich purple cupflower (Nierembergia 'Purple Robe') *and ethereal Heavenly Blue morning-glory. Bottom left are petunias in purple, lavender, rose, and pink.*

Most warm reds, oranges, and golds harmonize beautifully. Clockwise from top left are nasturtiums (Tropaeolum majus), *gerbera daisies* (Gerbera jamesonii), *French marigolds* (Tagetes patula), *and brilliant scarlet sage* (Salvia splendens). *The sage looks best surrounded with lots of green and white instead of other colors.*

Fragrance

Fragrant Annuals

Among the most fragrant annuals are agastache (Agastache *spp.*), *California poppy* (Eschscholzia californica), *sweet rocket* (Hesperis matronalis), *moonflower* (Ipomoea alba), *sweet pea* (Lathyrus odoratus), *Virginia stock* (Malcolmia maritima), *evening stock* (Matthiola longipetala), *blazing star* (Mentzelia lindleyi), *four-o'clock* (Mirabilis jalapa), *baby-blue-eyes* (Nemophila menziesii), *flowering tobacco* (Nicotiana *spp.*), *scented geranium* (Pelargonium *spp.*), *annual phlox* (Phlox drummondii), *mignonette* (Reseda odorata), *marigold* (Tagetes *spp.*), *blue lace flower* (Trachymene coerulea), *nasturtium* (Tropaeolum majus), *and verbena* (V. × hybrida).

*L*ouise Beebe Wilder, one of America's favorite garden writers, once wrote: "A garden full of sweet odors is a garden full of charm, a most precious kind of charm…which is beyond explaining." And a surprising number of annuals carry the gift of fragrance.

Fragrance can trigger more memories than any of the other senses. The smell of pinks *(Dianthus spp.)* on a summer's day could catapult your mind back to the last time you grew these flowers; the sweet, vanilla-like fragrance of heliotrope *(Heliotropium arborescens)* might remind you of the perfumes that were popular some years ago. As the sun sets, the light fragrance of evening stocks *(Matthiola longipetala)* will spread about the flowers, especially on still, warm nights, attracting not only gardeners but many of the moths that are the butterflies of the night.

As a rule, flowers with brilliantly colored petals are not often fragrant—they use their colors to attract pollinators. Usually the most fragrant flowers are either white or very light in color. And some of the sweetest, like mignonettes *(Reseda odorata)*, have dull flowers that are almost sad in their appearance. Then, too, the perfume is not always in the flowers but sometimes in the leaves.

Just remember that one gardener's pleasant scent is another gardener's vile odor. Some people love the fresh spicy smell of crushed geranium leaves and others abhor it. If visitors don't approve of one flower's smell, quickly lead them to another.

Garden flowers smell their best when the air is warm and the humidity reasonably high. Except with many of the herbs, the scent of flowers declines when the weather is very dry and hot. Fragrance always increases after a summer rain or shower from a garden sprinkler.

When using fragrant flowers try to put them close to pathways, so it isn't necessary to hop about the garden just to get a sniff of something beautiful. Be sure to plan a place to sit, to enjoy not only the many fragrances but also the butterflies, hummingbirds, and other creatures that will respond to the floral perfumes.

Don't forget to use fragrant flowers in bouquets, especially at the lunch or dinner table. And nothing beats a nosegay of sweet flowers as a house gift when visiting friends.

Deliciously fragrant sweet peas grow best where spring weather is cool and summer comes late or the weather gets hot gradually. Warm-climate gardeners can grow them in winter.

Long-Lasting Annuals

Many perennials have a short period of bloom. Globeflowers *(Trollius europaeus)*, peonies, and irises, for example, entertain for a month or less, then the show is over until the next year rolls around.

Not so with most annuals. Some begin to flower while still living in plastic packs at the garden center, then continue to bloom all summer, finally fading when the first frost comes around. And many annuals bloom without any attention from the gardener. Impatiens, nasturtiums, and marigolds shed their used blooms, then produce new ones, and would continue to do so even if nobody came to the garden. Other exuberant annual bloomers include zinnia, sweet alyssum, annual coreopsis *(C. tinctoria)*, fibrous begonia, rose mallow *(Hibiscus moscheutos)*, flowering tobacco *(Nicotiana* spp.*)*, spider flower *(Cleome hasslerana)*, salvia, woolflower *(Celosia cristata)*, Cape marigold *(Dimorphotheca* spp.*)*, verbena, ornamental pepper *(Capsicum annuum)*, lobelia, monkey flower *(mimulus* spp.*)*, rose moss *(Portulaca grandiflora)*, blue lace flower *(Trachymene coerulea)*, and periwinkle *(Vinca* spp.*)*.

All annuals benefit from deadheading, the somewhat macabre word for removing spent blossoms before seeds are formed. Thus the plant continues to send out chemical messages to produce more flowers.

Annuals that continue to bloom if dead flowers are removed include cosmos, dahlias, petunias (but pinch the stem, don't cut it off until reblooming has begun), geraniums, China pinks, snapdragons, gloriosa daisies, pansies (but they need cool weather), Swan River daisy *(Brachycome* spp.*)*, and wishbone flower.

Many of the mat-growing annuals like lobelias and alyssums also benefit from shearing, as long as the cutting is not too severe. Never remove more than the top third of the plants.

Finally, to guarantee a long period of bloom, careful gardeners resow annuals directly in the garden, but they usually wait until the weather begins to cool after the dog days of August.

White snapdragons, shown in the foreground of this garden, will often rebloom if you cut back the spent flower spikes.

These cheerful pots of annuals will bloom all summer long. The plantings include red, pink, and white geraniums with fragrant purple heliotrope.

Annuals in Containers

EARTH·WISE TIP

Buy bags of either sterilized all-purpose potting soil or topsoil and builder's or sharp sand (not beach sand because of the salt content). Thoroughly combine three-quarters of the soil with one-quarter of the sand to make a good mix for container gardens.

*E*ven if your garden consists of only a window ledge, you can have flowers blooming all summer long in anything from an old plastic pot to a noble terra-cotta container.

Tomb paintings from ancient Egypt depict earthenware pots being used for growing plants. Flowerpots from classical Greece—looking amazingly like present-day designs—held decorative plants and were used to root cuttings for eventual installation around temple borders.

In addition to saving space, container gardening is reasonably care-free. You must water annuals in containers—usually once a day and twice in hot weather, then fertilize every few weeks and deadhead spent blooms. But after these tasks are completed, you can usually sit back and relax.

Another beauty of container gardening is obvious when the first frosts of autumn arrive. You can cover your pots with garden "blankets" of spunbonded polyester or other light material, then in the warm days of Indian summer, your garden can continue to delight for weeks on end.

Almost any vessel that drains and will hold soil can be used to grow plants and flowers. Choices range from terra-cotta pots and tubs to clay pots, unglazed pottery, wire baskets lined with sphagnum moss, wooden or plastic window boxes, wine barrels cut in half, stone or concrete planters, old soapstone sinks, containers made of twisted vines and branches, metal urns, an old wheelbarrow, and as occasionally found here and there, old tires, possibly turned inside out.

A simple pot of red geraniums on a window ledge softens the lines of a dormer.

To create the effect of a garden in a single large container, combine plants of varying heights, textures, colors, and growing habits.

Window boxes overflowing with pansies and wallflowers (Cheiranthus cheiri) form a second-story planting above a mass of pink English daisies planted along the sidewalk.

Even jardinieres or antique pots without drainage holes can be used to show off flowers. Place a smaller plastic pot inside, remembering to set its bottom on a small clay saucer or a few small stones for proper drainage. If a drainless container is too large for a second pot, put gravel in the bottom to hold excess water, place a slim plastic pipe against the edge, then add soil. To tell if there is water at the bottom, insert a straw from a broom just as you use a dipstick to check the oil in your car.

Use earthenware pots whenever possible, washing them every fall so that you can use them again and again. If you do use plastic pots, place them inside more attractive containers or hide them behind the prettier pots.

Small plastic pots have a disadvantage because they are very light, especially when soil is dry, and easily blow over. Small pots are easy to move, however, and allow you great freedom to arrange them in pleasing combinations. When full of soil, especially wet soil, large pots can be heavy and very difficult to move, so take care when choosing a potential site.

Hanging pots save space and look marvelous screening a view. But thorough watering will result in dripping even in pots with saucers attached, so place these baskets where nothing will be damaged or unsightly after you've visited with the watering can.

Probably the most important consideration in matching a plant with an appropriate container is scale. A large decorative urn would look strange containing one small marigold.

This container combination works because the plant forms are varied and interesting together. The pot holds tall mealy-cup sage, dill, pink marguerite daisies, red and blue-violet petunias, and blue lobelia.

Pots of impatiens brighten a shady patio. The pink, white, and red flowers seem to peek out from every corner.

Playful morning-glories tumble out of a planter box attached to the railing of a deck and spill onto the ground.

Annuals in Containers CONTINUED

Basket Plants

Annuals that look great and trail properly for hanging baskets include browallia (B. speciosa), *Madagascar periwinkle* (Catharanthus roseus), *Queen Anne's pocket vine* (Cucumis melo), *Mexican cigar plant* (Cuphea platycentra), *Kenilworth ivy* (Cymbalaria muralis), *Persian violet* (Exacum affine), *lantana* (Lantana *spp.*), *flowering oregano* (Origanum rotundifolium), *ivy geranium* (Pelargonium peltatum), *rose moss* (Portulaca *spp.*), *purple bell vine* (Rhodochiton atrosanguineum), *nasturtium* (Tropaeolum majus), *black-eyed Susan vine* (Thunbergia alata), *and vinca* (V. major, V. minor).

Potted annuals along the steps and on the porch turn a shady front garden into a colorful oasis. For this kind of lush effect, group lots of potted plants together for masses of color.

Mixing plants in containers is mostly a matter of taste. The same so-called rules used in decorating a room are applicable to planting containers. Color intensity should match as well as environmental demands. Never put a succulent plant that gets by on little water in the same pot with water lovers like pansies or petunias—they will always be at odds.

Geraniums look great in clay or in wood. Bulbs are usually prettiest in clay pots. Many creeping plants really shine when set in stone or concrete containers.

Thin-leaved plants like ornamental grasses look best in airy containers, while plants with heavy, strap-like leaves call for stronger containers that look comfortable holding their weight. One strikingly beautiful and quite unusual combination is four or five pineapple lilies *(Eucomis bicolor)* in a large, elegant zinc urn, with masses of myrtle trailing over the edge.

Mixing Annuals and Perennials

One of the most valuable uses for annual plants is to mix them with perennials. Annuals are especially valuable for filling in spots where perennials like Virginia bluebells *(Mertensia virginica)* and Oriental poppies *(Papaver orientale)* have bloomed and vanished. Or you can employ them to fill the gaps left by slumbering spring bulbs like daffodils, narcissus, Spanish bluebells, or the great foxtail lilies *(Eremurus spp.)* when their foliage has ripened, browned, or been removed. Use annuals to screen early-blooming perennials like globeflower *(Trollius europaeus)* and cushion spurge *(Euphorbia polychroma)* so that when they finish flowering their unexciting forms will be screened by color.

Some annuals have so much solidity both in form and in flower structure that they look like perennials in size and habit. Spider flower *(Cleome hasslerana)* and bells-of-Ireland *(Moluccella laevis)*, for example, can be planted in areas surrounded by low-growing shrubs like boxwoods or hollies to give the appearance of a fully functional perennial garden. Annuals such as sunflower cultivars *(Helianthus annuus)* and Mexican sunflower *(Tithonia rotundifolia)* combine great height with strong stems and can easily be set in the midst of shorter perennials, where they act like colorful beacons in the garden.

Most perennial borders would not be able to provide color from late May to after frost without the use of annuals to fill in those missing spots of color. Flossflowers *(Ageratum houstonianum)* can be alternated with white petunias and planted in double rows with three plants every few feet so that the flowers

This gardener achieved season-long color in a subtle blue-and-white scheme with a masterful combination of annuals and perennials. Included are blue mealy-cup sage, tall white spider flower, white catharanthus, silvery dusty-miller, and perennial phlox.

Mixing Annuals and Perennials CONTINUED

TIMESAVING TIP

For a beautiful care-free mix of annuals and perennials, use two or three fountain grasses (such as Pennisetum alopecuroides 'Hamelyn'), *allowing 30 inches for each plant. In front plant a row of polka-dot plants* (Hypoestes phyllostachya) *set on 10-inch centers. This combination will last until a hard frost.*

swirl in and out rather than just marching along in a straight line. Masses of nasturtiums *(Tropaeolum majus)* are ideal for edging a vegetable garden; the cultivar 'Alaska Mixed', with its lovely pastel green foliage striped with cream, is particularly winning.

Cosmos are at home in almost any sunny garden. Both *Cosmos bipinnatus* 'Alba', with its graceful petals of white, and the shorter yellow cosmos *(C. sulphureus)*, are lovely mixed and massed in the midst of Siberian iris. The sword-shaped leaves of the iris are fitting foils for these pretty daisies that bloom all summer long until frost.

It isn't strictly accurate to call dahlias annuals, but that's the way they are usually grown (technically they are tender perennials). Their nonstop bloom, marvelous floral color, and variety of shapes make perfect additions to a flagging perennial garden. Dwarf dahlias are ideal as edging plants, while the larger cultivars can be either massed according to individual color or mixed with a definite color scheme in mind.

Geraniums (or pelargoniums) are also really perennials grown as annuals. Their flowering capabilities plus the endless cultivars that produce either interesting leaves or lovely colors for the flowers, or both, should show up in places other than window boxes or containers. Planted directly in the garden, they shine when mixed with plants that have finished with their flower production, like astilbe or German irises, or set between dwarf conifers.

1 *To create the look of a perennial garden, place a large number of annuals in curved drifts. Outline the drifts with lime or pieces of rope. Set plants at the correct spacing.*

Even annual ornamental grasses play their part, bringing texture more than color to the garden. Foxtail millet *(Setaria italica)* bears dense panicles that are often 1 foot long on 2- to 3-foot stems that gracefully bend with the weight of the seeds. Both the short and tall species of quaking grass *(Briza* spp.*)* when in bloom provide a grace that few perennials can exhibit. *B. maxima* grows between 2 and 3 feet tall, and little quaking grass *(B. minor)* is best in the front of the border, where its diminutive 1½-foot leaves topped with little seed heads that resemble puffed wheat are a delight to see.

2 When all the plants are in place, water them thoroughly. Keep the soil evenly moist—but not soggy—for the first week, while the plants become established in the soil.

3 Several weeks later the garden will be full of bright blossoms. If you don't like the way your design turns out this year, you can change it for next year's garden.

Annual opium poppies (Papaver somniferum), like this peony-flowered variety, look perfectly at home mixed in a perennial garden.

Cosmos daisies are lovely background plants with other annuals, perennials, or both.

Victoria salvia, grown as an annual north of zone 7, marries beautifully with perennials and blooms vigorously.

Snapdragons add vertical line to a mixed garden of annuals and perennials, and tall varieties add height.

Larkspur (Consolida ambigua) is another tall, elegant annual that combines well with perennials.

Regional Considerations

Warm-Weather Annuals

A selection of annuals for hot weather could include flowering maple (Abutilon spp.), love-in-a-puff (Cardiospermum halicacabum), cup-and-saucer vine (Cobaea scandens), California poppy (Eschscholzia californica), basket flower (Gaillardia pulchella), gazania (G. ringens), globe amaranth (Gomphrena globosa), strawflowers (Helichrysum bracteatum), New Guinea impatiens (Impatiens spp.), moonflower, red summer cypress (Kochia scoparia var. trichophylla), lantana, tree mallow (Lavatera trimestris), tidy-tips (Layia platyglossa), southern star (Oxypetalum caeruleum), poppies (Papaver spp.), gloriosa daisy (Rudbeckia hirta 'Gloriosa Daisy'), verbena, and vinca.

Because annuals are genetically programmed to complete their life cycle in one season, they usually have to withstand certain variable conditions. Three of the most important considerations are temperature tolerance, ability to withstand hot sunlight, and the amount of water each species requires.

Cool-weather annuals will do well throughout the country if planted when temperatures are pleasant, but they quickly burn out when the mercury rises to the uncomfortable range; the warmer the soil becomes the less they are able to tolerate the heat. But those annuals that revel in heat detest the cold and won't flower until soil temperatures have risen above 60° to 70°F. So don't expect to succeed with pansies where days and nights are torrid, and don't look for flowering tree mallows where the weather is cool and damp.

As to light intensity, many annuals that need full sun in New England and other northern locations would burn in the hot summer sun of southern California or the flatlands of the Southeast. They grow better with some shade in those locations. Surprisingly, some tropical plants like coleus and impatiens really need some afternoon shade in order to prosper in areas with intense sunlight.

Finally, there are annuals that will do very well on a limited diet of water and are good choices for hot, dry climates. For example, flowers like the Dahlberg daisy *(Dyssodia tenuiloba)* from south central Texas and northern Mexico, and the Cape marigold *(Dimorphotheca pluvialis)* from South Africa, come from areas associated with hot sun and often barren land and do quite well on short rations of water. Heat-tolerant plants frequently have fuzzy or scaled, often silvery leaves to offer protection from the sun, or their leaves are needle-thin in order to conserve as much moisture as possible.

Some of the best annual gardens can be found in the North, where long days and relatively cool summer temperatures encourage lavish, long-lasting bloom.

A romantic corner in a southeastern garden combines the exotic trumpets of Brugmansia *with hosta, chrysanthemum, and fragrant purple heliotrope.*

In warm-climate areas of the Southeast, Southwest, and West Coast, many annuals can be grown for winter flowers. This colorful winter garden contains orange poppies, multicolored pansies, purple stock, and verbenas.

Cutting Garden

rom late spring throughout summer and fall, this small garden provides enough continual blooms to supply bouquets for every room of your home.

The fence lends neatness and boundaries to this garden, which might otherwise appear a bit messy and unstructured.

You can sow most flowers directly from seed, although you can hasten the flowering season in northern climates by starting seeds indoors and transplanting them.

After the season is over, cut back all the stems and clean out the garden well in order to prevent pests and diseases from overwintering in the garden refuse. In the spring, turn over the soil and improve it by digging in compost or well-rotted manure. Experiment with different plant arrangements each year; the change is not only fun but also good for the soil.

Plant List

1 Snapdragon
(Antirrhinum majus)
2 Annual larkspur
(Consolida ambigua)
3 Cosmos
(Cosmos bipinnatus)
4 Dahlia
(Dahlia cultivars)
5 African daisy
(Arctotis stoechadifolia)
6 Annual baby's-breath
(Gypsophila elegans)
7 Swan River everlasting
(Helipterum manglesii)
8 Statice
(Limonium sinuatum)
9 Mealy-cup sage
(Salvia farinacea)
10 Zinnia
(Zinnia elegans)
11 Field poppy
(Papaver rhoeas)

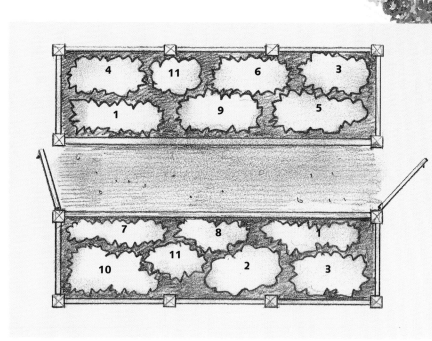

When you go to the garden to cut flowers, bring along some scissors or garden shears and a bucket of cool or tepid water. As you cut the flowers, immediately place the stems in water. Preventing the flowers from drying out will prolong the time that the blossoms stay fresh indoors. Don't be afraid to take too many blooms, since cutting back these plants helps to make them more vigorous and to prolong their flowering.

The beds in this cutting garden should be about 3 feet wide; if they are any wider, it is difficult to reach across to cut the farthest stems. If you want, you can create raised beds for easier access to the flowers. Be sure to plant the shorter varieties nearest the path and the taller ones in the back.

With a gate at each end, you can pull a wheelbarrow or a garden cart straight through the garden without having to try to turn it around. Keep the gates closed when no one is around—the fence will keep many animals out of the garden.

Tropical Paradise

*H*ere's a perfect garden for a small, narrow city lot. You'll feel transported to a faraway land when you retreat to this section of your backyard!

The plants here were chosen for their bright colors and strange, exotic shapes. For example, the big leaves of the caladium and the unusual form of the plumed cockscomb contribute to the sense of being in a tropical jungle. An existing tree provides support for the cardinal climber that runs up its trunk and then into the branches, creating a wild red canopy. The bright red is picked up in the big, splashy blossoms of the canna plants throughout the garden.

Plant List

1 Fancy-leaved caladium
(Caladium × hortulanum)
2 Canna
(Canna × generalis)
3 Musk mallow
(Abelmoschus moschatus)
4 Cabbage tree
(Cordyline australis)
5 Hyacinth bean
(Dolichos lablab)
6 Plumed cockscomb
(Celosia cristata Plumosa group)*
7 Impatiens
(Impatiens hybrids*)*
8 Weeping lantana
(Lantana montevidensis)
9 Japanese hops
(Humulus japonicus)
10 Cardinal climber
(Ipomoea × multifida)
11 Moonflower
(Ipomoea alba)

Even though the backyard of a city brownstone is not usually a spot that attracts a lot of wildlife, this garden will invite many species of birds and butterflies. The bright red blossoms will beckon hummingbirds, and the various green foliage plants will provide cover and shade for ground-feeding birds. By adding a small water feature or a birdbath, you will welcome even more birds to your tropical-looking garden.

Mailbox Garden

Why not turn an otherwise bare spot, the area around your mailbox, into a focal point surrounded by flowers from late spring through fall? This simple but charming garden plays up the cheery sunflower and morning-glory combination as a backdrop to the mailbox.

The yellow-and-blue color scheme is sustained throughout the garden. The sunflower look is echoed with the border of creeping zinnias, which look like miniature sunflowers; they will fill in nicely and even spill out over the wooden frame.

The plants chosen here are hardy enough to survive a mailbox location, which is apt to be in a hot, sunny spot that is sprayed with dirt and gravel from a nearby road as motorists pass.

Plant List

1 Blue marguerite
(Felicia amelloides)
2 Sunflower
(Helianthus annuus)
3 Morning-glory
(Ipomoea tricolor)
4 Mealy-cup sage
(Salvia farinacea)
5 Creeping zinnia
(Sanvitalia procumbens)
6 Edging lobelia
(Lobelia erinus)
7 Quaking grass
(Briza maxima)

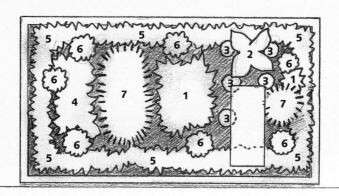

Sunflowers are fun to grow—the stems rise to more than 6 feet tall and are topped by large, heavy flower heads. If the site is windy or if the heads of the sunflowers are particularly heavy, you may need to provide stakes to support them. The morning-glories will grow up the mail post and then continue on up the nearby sunflower stalks.

The wooden frame surrounding this garden is an important feature. It acts as a curb and prevents a passerby from wandering over the plants. If you use 2-by-8s, you can bury the wood several inches into the ground and fill the whole bed with rich garden soil. Be sure to clean out the bed before winter and improve the soil with compost each year before planting in the spring.

Fragrance Garden

Day or night, here is a perfect retreat from the world. By day, the overhead trellis provides shade in which you can read a book or write a long overdue letter. By evening, the summer breezes mingle the fragrances of the many night-blooming flowers, creating a romantic spot to take in the moonlight.

Chosen for their scents, these flowers fill the air with their aromas, from the vanilla-scented heliotrope to the more subtle night-blooming flowering tobacco. This fragrant oasis delights the senses from early spring until frost.

Consider installing a few small outdoor lights in this garden. Many night-blooming flowers, such as moonflower and evening stock, are delightful to look at from indoors after the sun has set. If the garden is sufficiently well lit, you can weed it and pinch back and groom the plants in the cool of the evening instead of working on a sweltering afternoon.

You can buy a variety of ready-made garden furniture, arbors, and trellises to incorporate into this garden design. To save costs, consider using one of the many fine build-it-yourself kits that are available.

Plant List

1 Persian violet
(Exacum affine)
2 Heliotrope
(Heliotropium arborescens)
3 Japanese hops
(Humulus japonicus)
4 Sweet pea
(Lathyrus odoratus)
5 Sweet alyssum
(Lobularia maritima)
6 Evening stock
(Matthiola longipetala)
7 Stock
(Matthiola incana)
8 Flowering tobacco
(Nicotiana alata)
9 Mignonette
(Reseda odorata)
10 Moonflower
(Ipomoea alba)

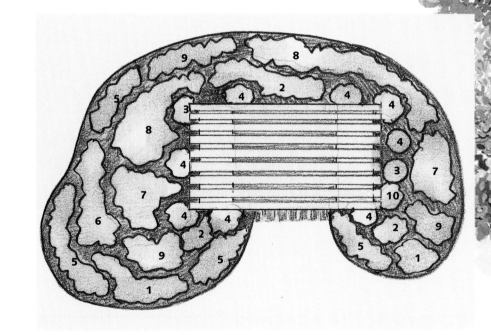

The sweet-pea vines may need additional help in order to climb up along the post. Try stringing a wire or a tight string along the post from top to bottom. The vine will be able to twine its tendrils around the string or wire and climb along it.

The hops do not need additional assistance since they are aggressive climbers, aided in their efforts by a sticky resinous secretion that helps the vine hold onto almost any surface.

CHAPTER 2

Managing the Garden Environment

One of the great things about gardening in your own backyard is the wonderful feeling that you get from being somewhat in control of something in a world where so much else seems to be slipping from your reach. • After all, if the soil around your house is poor and needs improvement, you can add compost or improve drainage. If rain doesn't fall, you can water. If water is scarce, you can fight dry conditions by choosing drought-tolerant plants and by using mulch. • If you garden in an area where frost comes early, cover chosen plants the night before it hits to extend the growing season well into autumn. A great deal is under the gardener's control.

Soil

If you turn your compost pile once a week and decomposition seems to be proceeding slowly, the ingredients may be too dry. A dry heap will not allow sufficient bacterial action to result in perfect compost. So if rainwater is not sufficient, you must occasionally add moisture. Spray the pile with a hose until the contents are as wet as a wrung-out sponge. Eventually the bacteria will break down the organic matter into a rich, dark brown humus that is completely free of odor but rich with benefits for your plants.

*B*ecause annuals complete their living requirements in one growing season, they can often tolerate less-than-perfect soil. But that doesn't mean that by punching a hole in solid clay and then planting seeds you can have annuals cheerfully blooming in the garden (although many annual weeds will).

The ideal garden soil is called loam. It contains clay and sand, plus organic matter and minerals. The more organic matter the soil contains, the better it is for plants. Loamy soil contains particles of organic matter that soak up water like a sponge but are separated by air spaces that allow plenty of oxygen to get to the roots and excess water to drain away.

Aeration is especially important because most plant roots (and most annuals) need both oxygen and water, from which they absorb nutrients to help them grow and bloom. In soils that are too dry or drain too quickly, there's not enough moisture for nutrients to be absorbed. When soil is too wet, plant roots—except on those plants specifically adapted to living in water—suffocate from lack of oxygen, then rot.

Sandy soil drains too quickly and robs plants not only of water, but in many cases of enough nutrients to allow plenty of bloom. To correct sandy soil, add lots of compost, including shredded leaves and aged livestock manure.

Clay soil is dense because it is made of tiny particles that stick together like glue. Clay soil drains slowly, feels sticky to the touch, and easily becomes waterlogged. Its dense texture makes it more difficult to dig than lighter soils. You can tell if your soil is clay because when wet, water will form pools on its surface and take a long time to drain away. To correct clay soil you must lighten its texture by adding plenty of organic matter. To improve drainage, you can also add sand, but be sure it's sharp or builder's

1 *To create an island bed in a lawn, first lay out its shape with stakes and string or a garden hose. Then remove the sod; push a spade horizontally under the sod and lift.*

sand and not fine beach sand. In many areas garden soil contains a substantial amount of clay.

Good garden soil contains plenty of organic material, and you can push in your shovel up to the hilt without hitting too much resistance.

Unfortunately, many gardeners—especially those who have typical subdivision lots—will find poor-quality soil in their backyards. Usually the builders have removed all the topsoil when digging foundations, and heavy equipment has compacted the soil that's left. But by adding more compost and improving drainage, you can develop a place that will soon grow beautiful flowers.

2 When the sod has been removed, add compost and other soil conditioners to the bed to improve texture. Dig or till the organic material into the soil.

3 Break up any large clods and clumps, and remove any big rocks. Then rake the soil smooth to create a finely textured planting area.

When planting, try to dig up your soil to at least the depth of a garden spade. Break up large clods of soil and remove large rocks and stones. Mix in the compost thoroughly, then rake the surface as smooth as you can. The photos on pages 52–53 illustrate how to do this.

And don't attempt to garden in a larger area than you can handle or you will become discouraged. Remember, gardening should be enjoyed and not approached with resentment. If you cannot produce great soil in one season, there's always next year— and the year after that.

Without a lot of fussing, pink and dark pink annual candytuft (Iberis umbellata), *white feverfew* (Tanacetum parthenium), *and perennial rose campion* (Lychnis coronaria) *put on a dazzling show in soil of average fertility.*

Light

Shade Lovers

Among the annuals suited for some shade are bedding begonias (Begonia × semper-florens-cultorum), *browallia, caladium, Madagascar periwinkle* (Catharanthus roseus), *coleus, hops* (Humulus japonicus), *polka-dot plant* (Hypoestes phyllostachya), *impatiens, monkey flower* (Mimulus × hybridus), *all the nicotianas, black-eyed Susan vine* (Thunbergia alata), *wishbone flower* (Torenia fournieri), *and pansies.*

A garden of sun-loving annuals in primary crayon colors contains red canna, blue Victoria salvia, and yellow marigold.

Most annuals like plenty of light—at least six hours of sun a day. One of the good things about living in the extreme northern United States or in Canada is the extra daylight in summer compared with the Deep South. All that sun stimulates annuals into voluminous blooming.

However, not all gardeners are lucky enough to have full sun shining on their flowers. Many of us have to contend with shade, and shade varies in quality and duration. From a gardener's perspective, shade can be divided into five basic types.

Light shade, also called open shade, is the kind of shade found beneath the leafy branches of a tall and stately tree. In the Northeast, Midwest, or Northwest, most common annuals need full sun in order to bloom well. As soon as you move south and the sun gets hot, however, annuals prefer light shade, especially in the afternoon.

Medium shade is found under a group of trees, where light is dappled as in the woods; you see reflected sunlight but not direct sunlight. Here impa-

TROUBLESHOOTING TIP

To let more light into a shady garden, try removing the lower branches of nearby trees. If the shade is still too dense to allow you much choice of plants, have an arborist selectively remove higher branches to lighten the canopy of leaves overhead.

Caladiums and begonias bring a splash of color and unique foliage to this shady spot.

tiens and other plants with a tropical heritage continue to bloom.

Full shade occurs when closely grouped trees and thickets combine to cut out direct sun and even bright, indirect light. While few plants will flower here, the secret is to grow them in pots. Let them bloom for a few weeks, then, before they get too leggy—in an attempt to reach for more light—move them to a sunnier spot. Then bring in another round of potted plants.

Deep shade is truly dark. In a deeply shaded garden the only successful alternative is to move in foliage houseplants for a few weeks at a time, then move them out to a brighter location.

Finally, seasonal shade occurs when the leaves of deciduous trees and shrubs begin to appear. In late winter and early spring, when the leaves are young and small, the sun is able to shine through, but as the summer advances and the leaves reach their full size, the shade deepens.

Moisture

While few common annuals do well in a wet spot, many tropical perennials that are treated as annuals thrive in boggy or wet conditions. Any of the so-called umbrella plants belonging to the genus Cyperus can be grown directly in water. The variegated umbrella plants are especially attractive in a garden setting.

When it comes to watering, the traditional rule of thumb is that gardens need 1 inch of water per week. Generally, if you are lucky enough to get a good soaking rain every seven days or so, you will probably not have to water. But remember that gardens with sandy soils and gardens at the seaside or in hot climates in general will need more water than gardens in the Northeast or Northwest. And containers, especially small ones, dry out quickly—in very hot weather they may need watering twice a day.

English daisies (Bellis perennis) *appreciate moist soil. They are perennials that bloom the first year from seed and are often grown as annuals.*

The best way to tell when the garden needs water is to stick your finger into the soil. If it feels dry a couple of inches below the surface, it's time to water.

Because annuals live for just one year, they do not have time to grow extensive root systems. This means that many annuals do poorly when not given adequate water. In order to get roots to grow as far down as they can, be sure to water deeply. If you forget to water and some of your plants wilt, don't give up too quickly. Many annuals will recover from water deprivation and go on to bloom with abandon.

There are a number of ways to get water to the garden when rainfall is insufficient. We have all seen advertisements showing a gardener happily sprinkling with a watering can. But except when you need water for transplants, this is not the way to go. There are many better ways of bringing water to your plants.

Overhead sprinklers are the least efficient of all, especially in areas of high sun, high heat, and porous soil. Unfortunately, overhead sprinklers are all many of us have. If you use them, remember to water early in the morning or late in the afternoon. Wet foliage at night can invite disease, but watering at night is still better than not watering at all. Except in areas where the atmosphere is always as humid as a tropical rainforest, your plants will not rot away if watered at night. After all, it often rains at night, too. And try not to water on very windy days, because too much of the moisture will evaporate.

California poppies (Eschscholzia californica) *tolerate dry conditions and hot sun.*

Annuals for Dry Places

Annuals for dry conditions include prickly poppy (Argemone *spp.*), *Swan River daisy* (Brachycome iberidifolia), *cosmos* (C. bipinnatus *and* C. sulphureus), *tassel flower* (Emilia javanica), *California poppy* (Eschscholzia californica), *gazania* (G. ringens), *globe amaranth* (Gomphrena globosa), *strawflower* (Helichrysum bracteatum), *Mexican tulip poppy* (Hunnemannia fumariifolia), *red summer cypress* (Kochia scoparia *var.* trichophylla), *tree mallow* (Lavatera trimestris), *blazing star* (Mentzelia lindleyi), *opium poppy* (Papaver somniferum), *gloriosa daisy* (Rudbeckia hirta 'Gloriosa Daisy'), *rose moss* (Portulaca grandiflora), *and immortelle* (Xeranthemum annuum).

When buying a hose for the garden, don't stint! Cheap hoses quickly wear out, especially when left in a tangled heap out in the hot sun or thrown in the corner of the garage for the winter months.

Today, better watering begins with a soaker hose. It looks like a regular garden hose but has tiny holes that let water ooze slowly out to soak the ground with little loss to evaporation. Soaker hoses and plastic drip-irrigation tubing can be installed under ground, under mulch, or placed on top of the soil. Kits are available that provide all the parts that you will need.

If you hook drip-irrigation systems or soaker hoses to a timer, the water will turn on even when you're away on vacation.

Temperature

Cool-Weather Annuals

Annuals that bloom beautifully in cool weather include the common pansy (Viola × wittrockiana), a plant that does well as long as the ground doesn't freeze. There are other annuals that thrive in cool weather, including snapdragon, calendula, bachelor's-button (Centaurea cyanus), most of the annual chrysanthemums, California poppies, blanket flowers (Gaillardia pulchella), annual stocks (Matthiola incana 'Annua'), Phlox drummondii, most of the salvias, sweet alyssum (Lobularia maritima), the verbenas, and the sleepy daisy (Xanthisma texana).

*J*ust like people, some annuals like cool weather, while others love it as hot as it can get. Pansies, for example, will happily bloom even if they are exposed to frost every night, but coleus will simply shrivel up and die. In the introduction to this book we defined the three types of annuals—hardy, half-hardy, and tender (see pages 6–9).

Hardy annuals tolerate a reasonable degree of frost. Even in colder areas of this country, many will live through the winter as small seedlings, the result of fall plantings (sown by hand or from self-sown seeds). Their seeds will also survive a winter outside and germinate the following spring. You can sow seeds of hardy annuals in fall or in early spring as soon as the soil can be worked. Late spring frosts will not harm hardy annuals.

Half-hardy annuals are damaged, set back, or killed by exposure to a hard frost, but most will withstand an occasional light frost and thrive in cool, even wet weather. Plant half-hardy annuals in spring, after the ground in your garden has thawed and will not freeze again.

Tender annuals are usually from the tropics. They need warm soil for their seeds to germinate and are immediately killed by frost (although it's surprising how some roots will survive). Tender annuals grow best when the weather stays warm.

Today most seed company catalogues comment on heat tolerance when they describe their plants. Obviously, those catalogues do not know where you live. If you garden in the North, you must start seeds of many annuals indoors and move the plants to the garden after all danger of frost is past in order to guarantee that the plants will bloom before being struck down by an early fall frost. The frost-free growing season is simply too short to permit seeds of most annuals to be sown directly in the garden. If you live in the hotter parts of the country, you can sow many plants directly, but make sure you choose heat-resistant annuals for your garden.

Cool-weather annuals start blooming in spring in northern gardens and make excellent winter flowers in warm climates. Shown here are, top left to right, calendulas, pansies, and sweet alyssum; and bottom, sweet peas and Canterbury-bells.

A romantic combination of annuals that hold up well in hot weather includes white cosmos, pink spider flower, blue salvia, and the soft plumes of an ornamental grass, Hordeum jubatum.

Most warmth-loving annuals will survive in somewhat cooler conditions if their soil is not too cold. If you plan to grow warm-season annuals in the North, use a soil thermometer to find out when the soil is warm enough to set them out. Until then, keep seedlings in a protected spot and utilize a soil-heating cable to guarantee acceptable temperatures.

CHAPTER 3

Growing Annuals

*f*ew things warm a gardener's heart as much as the arrival of seed catalogues on a cold and blustery winter day. After looking at all those colored pictures of the newest cultivars developed by the plant breeders, most gardeners get the urge to run out into the cold and begin to dig. • So why look at mail-order seed catalogues except to torture ourselves in winter? Can't we get everything we need at the local garden center? • The answer is a qualified yes. You can indeed get plenty of annuals for your garden at local outlets, but you will never find the range of choices offered in seed catalogues—and you will never beat the cost savings when you grow annuals from seed.

Starting Seeds Indoors

*T*o get a jump on the growing season, you can start many annual seeds indoors. Look through seed catalogues and make your selections early in the new year (see pages 128–129 for a list of seed companies that specialize in annuals). Ordering early is important, because companies often run out of desirable varieties of seeds. When your seeds arrive, sort the packages by those to be planted immediately, those best started about eight to ten weeks before your last frost, and seeds to be planted directly outdoors in the spring.

For those seeds that must be stored for a month or so, place the packets in a closed glass jar in the refrigerator—not in the freezer. Most of the bigger seed companies now use foil-wrapped vacuum-sealed packages, but many smaller firms cannot afford such sophisticated packaging equipment, so you must refrigerate the seeds to keep them cool and dry.

When you are ready to start germinating the seeds, you will need a growing mix, and containers to hold the mix. If you do not have a warm spot in the house where the temperature is always above 65°F, you will benefit from a heating cable.

Containers for starting seeds are made of plastic, pressed peat moss, and pressed fiber. They usually come in round or square pots, 2¼ inches or 3 inches wide. Or you can use old (but clean) containers from frozen orange juice, cut-down milk cartons, or even foil pans from frozen dinners.

A light, porous growing medium that retains moisture but does not get waterlogged is important for starting seeds indoors. A number of prepared mixes are now available. These commercial preparations are especially valuable because the messy job of mixing ingredients has already been done and the media are sterile—an important consideration when starting your own seeds.

1 *Many annuals can be started indoors from seed to get a jump on the growing season. Begin by filling flats or other containers with moist potting mix.*

4 *Immediately after planting, label each flat or group of pots with the plant name and, if you are planting different varieties of the same plant, the color as well.*

2 *Sow the seeds by scattering them evenly over the surface of the medium, seeding in rows, or for larger seeds, by placing individual seeds.*

3 *You can also plant larger seeds in individual pots to minimize thinning and transplanting later. Sow two or three seeds in each pot; later eliminate all but the sturdiest seedling.*

Recycled containers for starting seeds indoors include, clockwise from front, eggshells, undivided seed trays, and cell packs from the garden center. Cover with plastic to maintain high humidity until seeds germinate.

5 *Cover plants with plastic to hold in humidity until the seeds germinate. Keep the containers out of direct sun, and open the cover each day to let in fresh air.*

Starting Seeds Indoors CONTINUED

TROUBLESHOOTING TIP

Remember to read the packet instructions or check the seed catalogue when working with seeds that are covered with a hard coating. Many well-protected annuals germinate much faster when the seed coat is nicked with a file or the seeds are soaked in warm water for up to 24 hours. And don't forget that some seeds must have light to germinate.

Most gardeners have problems when starting plants from seed because the growing mix is too cold. Many plants will germinate at temperatures below 50°F, but most annuals do much better when provided with gentle bottom heat from a heating cable. Cables are sold in lengths from 12 to 120 feet. A 12-foot cable, which heats an area of 4 square feet, uses the power of a 40-watt light bulb.

To begin sowing seeds, first wet your growing mix. Next fill your containers, leaving about ¼ inch of space at the top, and pat down the mix.

The individual seed packets will tell you how deep to plant the seeds and whether light is needed for germination. But if you have no directions, cover seeds ¹⁄₁₆ inch or larger by the thickness of one seed. You need not cover tiny seeds, like those of begonias; just settle them in with a light spray of water.

When sowing smaller seeds, cut off the top of the seed packet, squeeze the sides together, then gently tap the packet with your finger while moving it across the surface of the growing mix to scatter the seeds. Sometimes it's easier to tap out the seeds from a folded piece of paper.

Once the seeds are planted, cover the containers to prevent the mix from drying out (plastic kitchen wrap works very well). The soil must never dry out once the germination process has started.

Don't forget to label each pot with the name of the plant and the date of sowing.

After seeds begin to germinate and the first green shoots appear, move the containers into the sunlight or under one of the special lighting fixtures available to illuminate seed flats. Remove the plastic cover and check on moistness every day. When the mix starts to

When indoor-grown seedlings are hardened off, you can transplant them to the garden. A wheelbarrow comes in handy if you have lots of plants.

1 *When seedlings in undivided flats become crowded, transplant them to individual pots. Gently lift the seedling from the soil, supporting it with a plant label or pencil.*

2 *Set each seedling in a pot of moist potting mix, and gently firm soil around the roots. In several weeks the plants will be ready to transplant out in the garden.*

dry, carefully water the seedlings with room-temperature water, never with cold water. The photographs on pages 62–63 illustrate how to sow seeds indoors.

After seedlings develop their first true leaves (the ones with the shape characteristic of the plant), begin using a mild liquid fertilizer, especially if your growing mix does not contain added nutrients. Follow package directions, and do not overfeed.

As the seedlings grow you will eventually need to move them to larger containers. If seedlings are crowded in large flats or bigger containers, thin them out, leaving at least 1 inch between plants. Or prick them out and move them to individual containers.

The pointed end of a clean knife, a plastic plant label, or even a sharpened tongue depressor makes an excellent tool for transplanting. But be gentle. Carefully pick up the seedling by holding onto one of its

leaves, move it to the new container, then lightly cover the roots with soil that is damp but never mucky. See the photographs above illustrating how to transplant crowded seedlings.

Good air circulation, sterile growing media, and clean equipment are the best safeguards against damping-off—a fungal disease usually associated with unsterilized dirt. The moist conditions needed to germinate seeds encourage the fungus to grow. As seedlings emerge from the soil, the fungus attacks and fells the tender new stems.

There are four guidelines to follow to ensure proper germination of seeds: Do not overwater seed containers, but never let the mix completely dry out. To water tiny seedlings use a mister so that the mix is not disturbed. Never sow seeds too deeply. Keep seeds out of direct sunlight until germination is complete.

Planting Seeds Outdoors

Growing seedlings for eventual planting out in the garden is a great way to expand your collection of annuals. If you want to plant large areas of the garden with sweeps of color, however, direct seeding is the best method.

There are two time-honored methods used for growing seeds outdoors. Both require crumbly, fine-textured soil, which you can create by working up your garden soil, breaking up clods and clumps, then raking it level. Next, use the edge of a regular hoe, a gooseneck hoe, or even the edge of a board to make reasonably straight furrows of the appropriate depth for the seeds you are planting. Now, scatter the seeds in the furrows and cover them lightly with soil. Firm the soil with the flat of the hoe or the board, then water carefully so that the seeds are not dislodged. Use the fine-spray setting on the garden hose or, for a small garden, a watering can. Mark the end of each row with a label, and remember to keep watering whenever the soil becomes dry. When the seedlings emerge, you can thin them out and use the extras in other parts of the garden.

For a more informal look, you can broadcast, or scatter, the seeds over the prepared soil in a random manner. If you use this method, be on the lookout for weeds that may emerge and be confused with seedlings.

Most of the larger annuals benefit from direct seeding, especially those with taproots—such as poppies—as these plants often perish because of transplanting.

▼ Hardening Off

The process of adjusting plants to their new outdoor environment is called hardening off. Just as human skin has to adjust slowly to the summer sun, the thin tissue on plant leaves must be given a chance to thicken in order to adjust to the wind and weather of the outdoor garden. It is especially necessary when plants are brought from a greenhouse, cold frame, or any environment where they have been shielded from the elements.

About a week before the best time for transplanting, gather your seedlings on the front porch or in a protected part of the garden. You could even let them sit out in the garden proper, with a simple screen or piece of shade cloth positioned overhead.

If you garden where there is usually a danger of late frost, you can make a temporary cold frame to harden off plants. Some old storm windows set atop a base of cinder blocks will serve adequately. Ventilation is guaranteed by air moving freely through the open sides of the blocks.

1 Fast-growing annuals can be directly seeded. Prepare the soil and mark out the planting pattern on the soil with lime or lengths of rope.

2 Scatter (or broadcast) a different type of annual seed in each section of the prepared bed or border.

3 Label each planting area with the name of the plant. Labeling will help you identify young seedlings and distinguish them from weeds.

4 Firm the soil gently over the newly planted seeds, without burying them too deeply. Most seeds germinate when just pressed into the soil.

5 Water the seeds well immediately after planting. Use a fine spray of water that will not dislodge the seeds or wash them away.

Transplanting

When transplanting seedlings and nursery plants to the garden, try to pick a dull or cloudy day. If the sun is shining, aim for early morning or, second best, late afternoon. If the soil is dry, water it a few hours before you begin.

Make sure the seedling roots never dry out, and keep the plants in the shade until you can plant them. Try to work quickly if the sun is hot.

Before transplanting seedlings check the seed packets to see how far apart the plants should be spaced. Never crowd seedlings. They will probably look like a bit of green in a sea of brown at first, but they will soon spread out and fill in the gaps.

If the seedlings are growing in individual pots, you might find it helpful to set them out in the planting area while still in their pots, to try out different configurations. Remember, to get the most visual impact from your plants, place them in odd-numbered groups (five, seven, nine, or more) in a small garden, or plant in flowing drifts in a larger garden. If you are planting a carpet bed or other formal bed, you may want to use a yardstick or measuring tape to lay out precise planting patterns. When you have found a pleasing arrangement you can begin to plant.

As you plant, keep a watering can nearby, full of tepid—not cold—water. Dig a hole, then fill it with water. When the water soaks in add more, then put the seedling in place, firmly patting the soil around the crown of the plant. In most cases it's a good idea to add a water-soluble fertilizer, mixed at half strength, to the watering can.

Remove a plant from its container. If the plant does not slide easily from the pot, tap the bottom and sides with the handle of a trowel to loosen it, or lay the pot on its side and press on it while rolling it back and forth a few times. If the plant looks root-bound, either pull the roots apart with your fingers or cut them apart with a sharp utility knife. Draw the blade of the knife down one side, across the bottom, then up the opposite side of the rootball. Cut about one-third of the way into the rootball. Don't worry about cutting roots in this way; new ones will quickly grow.

When moving plants from cell packs purchased at the garden center, be sure to first remove any damaged stems or leaves.

An overcast day is best for transplanting. If the sun is hot, cover new transplants with a piece of shade cloth or spunbonded polyester for a few days to ease their transition into the garden. The cloth shades the transplants while their roots get acclimated to their new home and keeps soil moisture from evaporating too quickly.

1 Transplant seedlings of tender plants like impatiens to the garden after all danger of frost is past. Space them properly; the garden will look empty at first, but will fill in.

2 At the garden center, buy compact, stocky seedlings like the one on the right. Avoid lanky seedlings with widely spaced leaves, like the plant on the left.

3 Impatiens are classic shade plants. As a change from massing impatiens under a tree, create a small raised bed of assorted plants, with impatiens along the outer edges.

4 Cool green perennial hostas and ferns combine beautifully with impatiens in assorted warm tones in a charming little shade garden.

Plant-Shopping Tips

When shopping for annuals, remember that the best buy is not always the most beautiful plant.

Check that all the plants are watered, not dried out or shriveled, and that shade-loving annuals are kept under a sunscreen.

When choosing container plants, look for healthy, young foliage that is not burned and broken. Leaves should be green, not yellow; yellow leaves show signs of starvation.

Pop a plant out of its pot and see how tight the roots are growing. You want to see healthy roots winding through visible planting medium—not a solid mass of roots. Although tightly rooted plants can be untangled, when transplanted they are never as successful as younger plants.

Choose plants that have a lot of buds, but not flowers, and plants that are low and bushy, not tall and straggly. When buying cell packs (six or more plants growing in the same container), make sure that all six are straight and healthy.

Planting in Containers

Drainage, soil composition, watering, and pot size are important to consider when growing plants in the confines of containers. If pots do not drain properly, the soil soon becomes waterlogged and plant roots rot. The potting mix should allow free passage of water but contain plenty of organic matter.

Because the container is exposed to open air on all sides, the soil will quickly dry out, especially in the hot sun. Frequent watering is needed, but organic materials and minerals are rapidly leached out of the soil and must be replaced.

Be sure to choose an appropriate-size pot. Pots that are too small easily topple over in the wind and may be out of scale with the burgeoning annuals they hold.

Preblended potting media are available, most of them soilless peat-based mixes. Many gardeners find these packaged mixes too light for most container gardening and prefer to make their own. Start with a good bagged potting soil, top soil, or regular garden soil. Mix one-half of whatever soil you choose with one-half sharp builder's (not beach) sand and, if you have it handy, throw in a few handfuls of vermiculite. Don't use peat moss; it's difficult to get wet and is not a good growing medium.

Cover the pot's drainage hole with a bit of screening or a pot shard to keep the soil from coming out. Add enough mix to half-fill the container, position the new plant, put more potting mix around it, and carefully firm the soil. Leave an inch of space open at the top of the container to make watering easier.

When the plants are in place, water well. This helps to settle the soil around the new plants and eliminate air pockets. If hollows develop, add more soil to level the surface. Keep newly planted containers out of the hot sun for a few days, so the annuals can settle in.

Pots of daisies and pansies dance alongside brick steps. If you have annuals left over after planting your garden, try putting them in containers and massing the containers to create a "garden" in an unexpected place.

1 Annuals look great planted in a strawberry jar. First fill the jar to the lowest pocket with moist potting medium that is light and crumbly but moisture-retentive.

2 To help plants adjust more readily if weather is not ideal at planting, clip off flowers. Plants will form new buds as soon as the roots establish themselves.

3 Set one plant into each pocket, then add soil to cover the roots. Firm the soil gently. It's easiest if you start with the lowest pocket and work your way up the jar.

4 When all the side pockets are planted, plant in the top of the jar. Again, to ease the adjustment for plants, clip off flowers already in bloom.

Planting in Containers CONTINUED

When growing annuals in containers, remember that a lightweight plastic pot can be made heavier by adding a few large stones to the bottom of the pot before you add the soil. Also, put a small flat stone on top of the soil to deflect the stream of water that comes out of a watering can, and to prevent a hole from developing in the dirt.

1 To plant a container that will be viewed from all sides, fill the planter with a good, moist potting mix. Plant the tallest plants in the center of the container.

2 Place the plants that will grow next tallest on both sides of the container (or just along the front, if the container will be viewed from only one side).

1 If you want to plant in a wooden tub or half barrel, you can extend the life of the container by lining it with plastic before filling it with moist potting mix.

2 For an effective display, use plants of different heights. Plant the tallest plants first. Put them in the center of a freestanding tub that will be seen from all sides.

3 Continue by planting the next largest plants. Work your way out toward the edge of the container with plants of decreasing size.

4 Keep the container well watered. In hot, dry weather, window boxes and planters will need watering every day or even twice a day if the containers are small.

3 Working outward toward the outer edges of the container, put in the medium-size plants next and put in the smallest plants last.

4 Finally, plant trailing vines, such as the variegated vinca (V. major 'Variegata') shown above, to spill over the sides of the tub.

Watering

Chapter Two discussed the importance of water in the entire garden and the equipment used to apply it. This page covers watering new plants that have yet to establish the all-important root system so necessary for exuberant growth and proper flowering.

Check your new transplants every day, especially if the sun is hot, the air is warm, and there is a notice-able breeze or wind. The warm air moving over the open ground will quickly absorb water, sometimes leaving the plant roots in dire straits. New trans-plants need soil that is evenly, constantly moist, but not soggy.

When planting small peat pots directly into the soil (a practice often used with annuals that may not sur-vive root disturbance), be sure that no part of that pot protrudes above the soil. If it does, the dry peat will act like a wick, soaking water from the soil and let-ting it evaporate into the air.

If you water the new plants with a watering can, turn the rose at the tip so that the holes point upward to the sky instead of down toward the earth. This allows the water to pour out in a gentler flow and minimizes soil disturbance.

Finally, remember that a little bit of water is fre-quently worse than no water at all. When you water, do so thoroughly, letting the moisture soak into the ground where the roots need it—don't merely wet the surface.

1 *If you water annuals from overhead, do so early enough in the day that the foliage dries before nightfall. A water-ing-wand hose attachment provides a gentle spray.*

2 *Drip-irrigation tubing and soaker hoses use water more efficiently than overhead sprinklers, and are very handy if flowers are planted in rows or blocks.*

Pinching and Deadheading

Your thumb and forefinger are among the best gardening tools you have. These two fingers can be especially effective in pinching back young plants to encourage bushier growth and, eventually, more flower buds. Pinching back young plants causes them to redirect their energy into sending out more side shoots instead of growing taller. Many plants can double in width after they have been pinched back.

The thumb and forefinger also come in handy for one of the most important garden chores—deadheading. Simply put, deadheading is removing spent blossoms before they can begin to produce seeds, or removing developing seed heads before they mature.

Despite its unfortunate name, it's not an unpleasant activity, and can actually be a source of relaxing, contemplative time spent in the garden. It's best to deadhead on a bright, sunny day when it's enjoyable to be outdoors, rather than on a day when skies are gloomy and rain threatens.

When most flowers are finished blooming, they manufacture a chemical messenger that informs the rest of the plant that pollination is complete and flowers are ready to begin the process of seed production. If you remove the flower that is in transformation or the burgeoning seedpod, another message is broadcast. This message signals failure to produce seeds,

1 *Cut back snapdragons after the first flush of bloom wanes; they will often flower again later in the season.*

2 *In several weeks the snapdragons will produce a whole new round of flowers.*

Pinching and Deadheading CONTINUED

1 *Sweet alyssum grows best in cool weather. If your plants slow or stop blooming in summer heat, shear them back with hedge clippers or grass shears.*

2 *A few weeks after you have sheared the plants back, you will see the sweet alyssum begin to bloom again with renewed vigor.*

and plants send up a second round of bloom. Because annuals must complete their entire life cycle in one season, they are driven to bloom and set seeds. That's why annuals usually respond to deadheading with far more gusto than the majority of perennials.

Some of the more floriferous annuals, such as bedding begonias, impatiens, cleomes, many nicotianas, and most morning-glories, will deadhead themselves; their old blossoms will dry and shrivel, soon falling to the ground of their own accord. Other plants, such as cosmos, zinnias, and annual blanket flowers, will appreciate your grooming efforts, quickly produce more blossoms, and look a great deal better in the long run.

Some annual plants, such as coleus, produce flowers that are far less attractive than their foliage. Those flowers should literally be nipped in the bud to keep new leaves in production and give a neat look to the plants.

1 *Coleus plants produce slender spikes of small purple flowers that detract from the appearance of the plants.*

2 *Pinch off the flower spikes between your thumb and forefinger, back to the uppermost set of leaves.*

3 *After pinching, coleus plants look much neater and meld better with nearby plants.*

Nasturtiums bloom all summer and need little or no dead-heading. The flowers and leaves are edible, too.

Weeding and Mulching

People who do not like gardening often cite the unpleasant activity of weeding to make their case. Most gardeners disagree, pointing out that weeding is one of the few jobs that lets you easily see where you began, know just how long it took to finish, and actually get a feeling of accomplishment when the job is over. Weeding offers a good excuse to spend time among your flowers.

Just one warning: Mark seedling plants clearly when they come up so that you are able to distinguish between the soon-to-be-strapping weed and the long-awaited flower.

If you have neither the time nor the temperament for weeding, you can mulch the garden instead. Proper mulching accomplishes three things: It severely cuts back on the growth and germination of weeds; it helps to retain moisture in the soil by slowing the rate of evaporation; and a well-laid mulch is far more attractive in a formal garden than a wide expanse of seemingly unused dirt.

Garden centers sell a variety of mulches, including pine bark chips, marble chips, pine needles, pecan hulls, cocoa bean hulls (which smell like chocolate), and black plastic. Don't use peat moss to mulch the garden; once dry, it actually repels water, and the soil underneath can become dangerously dry. The use of black plastic is an aesthetic choice. Plastic does hold in water and cuts back on weed growth, but many gardeners abhor the way it looks.

There are also commercial mulches that include various mixes of organic materials, often laced with pleasant-smelling cedar chips.

Scarlet runner beans (Phaseolus coccineus) *reward the gardener with lovely flowers and edible beans. In this garden they grow in well-mulched raised beds set among neat pathways covered with mulch, which prevents splashing mud and keeps shoes clean.*

Fertilizing

When perennials bloom poorly or produce little or no seed, they can try again the next year—but annuals do not get a second chance. And because annuals work hard to form flowers, gardeners want to help them put on the best show possible.

Like other plants, annuals need the big three nutrients—nitrogen, phosphorous, and potassium—along with smaller amounts of secondary nutrients such as magnesium and calcium, and minute quantities of trace elements, including boron and iron. Healthy soil, rich in organic matter, provides the basic nutrition most plants need and usually contains adequate amounts of trace elements and secondary nutrients. In organically rich soils you can probably grow many annuals without supplemental fertilizers. But at times adding compost is not enough. Some annuals want more nutrients, especially if they are grown in pots. Every time water drains through the hole at the bottom of the container, nutrients in the soil are carried along with it, and they should be replaced.

In addition to incorporating organic amendments into the garden soil each year, give periodic applications of fertilizers containing all three major nutrients to ensure that your annuals are well nourished. If a soil test shows your soil is deficient in secondary or trace minerals, supply those as well (USDA and private soil-testing laboratories will instruct you on what to add to bring the nutrients up to acceptable levels).

For flowering annuals, use an all-purpose plant food, such as a 5-10-5 or 10-10-10 formula. Flowering plants have special need of phosphorous and potassium to realize their blooming potential. Foliage plants will flourish with a formula higher in nitrogen (the first of the three numbers in a fertilizer formula).

Whatever type of fertilizer you choose—granular or liquid, synthetic or organic—follow the directions on the package for how much to use and how often to apply it. Overfertilizing is worse for plants than feeding them too little. Too much fertilizer causes rapid, weak growth that is susceptible to damage by pests and diseases, and excess fertilizer runs off and may find its way into the water table, causing pollution.

For annuals in beds and borders, granular fertilizers are one option. Spread granular fertilizers over the soil around the plants and scratch them in lightly. Then water. You can apply synthetic granular fertilizers at planting time and periodically throughout the growing season. It takes more time for the nutrients in organic fertilizers to become available to plants, so these fertilizers are usually applied in spring before planting. Rock powders such as phosphate rock and granite dust, which organic gardeners use to supply phosphorus and potassium to the soil, break down very slowly and should be added in fall to nourish plants in next year's garden.

Liquid fertilizers are ideal for potted plants. Years ago, committed organic gardeners made manure tea by steeping fresh manure in water, eventually producing a dark brown liquid. Manure tea works like a wonder, but it's not a pleasant way to accomplish the job. Today there are a number of liquid fertilizers on the market that are environmentally safe yet contain the nutrients needed to ensure good plant growth. One of the best is a concentrate called fish emulsion, but be sure you look for the deodorized form, especially if you ever plan to use it indoors.

You can follow the instructions on the package or dilute the concentrate to half the recommended strength. A half-strength solution saves money while providing adequate nourishment. It also keeps you from overfertilizing plants. Apply liquid fertilizer every three or four weeks, especially to potted plants.

Fertilizing CONTINUED

1 *Compost is a good way to recycle plant debris and some kitchen wastes. Make a simple pen with wooden posts and chicken wire or hardware cloth.*

2 *You can even make compost in a metal garbage can. Drill holes around the bottom for aeration, and fill the can with alternate layers of kitchen wastes and shredded leaves.*

3 *A convenient compost container is a wood bin with slatted sides. Make one side of the bin easily removable or hinged, so that it is simple to turn the pile once a week.*

4 *You can also make compost without a bin or pen. The pile will be smaller and will not heat up as much as a contained pile, but you will still end up with lots of humus.*

Stakes and Supports

Many annuals are neat and tidy in their growth and habit. They amble along the ground or form low mounds of flowers and foliage that are always attractive, even after a heavy summer rainstorm.

Some plants grow tall and straggly. Without the help of a few well-placed stakes or some string, their stems flop about, giving a decidedly untidy look to the garden.

Pea-staking is an ancient method of holding up plants. Branches pruned from trees are spread about and plants grow up between the twigs, eventually covering them with foliage. (The term "pea-staking" originated in English vegetable gardens, where such natural stakes were used to hold up pea vines.)

A cat's cradle results from winding green garden twine back and forth and diagonally across four wooden or bamboo stakes set at the corners of a plot. The photo below shows using a cat's cradle to support larkspur. The photo on page 82 shows a tepee support.

Bamboo stakes (both real and plastic) or thin but straight wooden stakes can be used to support single-stemmed plants. Use special plastic clips, bits of string, or twist ties to hold the stems fast.

Many garden supply catalogues now offer interlocking stakes made of a green plastic-coated wire, which can be formed in many shapes, from a simple square to a long, spiral "S." And loops of the

Tall plants like these larkspur may need staking to keep the stems upright. A good way to support a group of plants like these is to hammer a series of stakes into the ground and wind string or yarn around and among them in a cat's cradle.

Stakes and Supports CONTINUED

same plastic are now sold that ride up and down straight supports, enabling the loops to grow with the plants.

Climbing annuals, such as morning-glories, cup-and-saucer vine *(Cobaea scandens),* hops *(Humulus* spp.), sweet peas *(Lathyrus odoratus),* and scarlet runner bean *(Phaseolus coccineus),* need tall, vertical supports. You can grow most of these plants on trellises, latticework, or a series of vertical strings, as described below. Hop vines are heavier and need a sturdy support. Train hops on a tripod made of wooden poles lashed together at the top or on a stout trellis or arbor. Hop vines are excellent for shading a porch, and their large leaves make them a good choice to cover a dilapidated shed or to screen the compost pile from view.

Trellises for other climbing annuals can take a variety of forms. They may be either freestanding or placed against a wall. Flat trellises are usually made of wood strips that are arranged in lattice patterns, fans, or geometric shapes. You can buy them or build your own.

If your front porch is enclosed by a wooden railing, you can plant morning-glories or other thin-stemmed vines to screen, shade, and decorate the porch. Screw a series of small metal hooks (like the ones sold to hang coffee cups), spaced at regular intervals, into the railing and the roof above, then tie string or fishing line beween the hooks. Plant the vines in pots or rectangular planters, so their stems can climb the strings.

Fragrant sweet peas need a support to climb. You can train them on strings or grow netting, and they will also happily climb a tepee made of wooden poles lashed together.

Cutting Gardens

*F*or gardeners dedicated to filling their homes with freshly cut flowers, every house or apartment offers an opportunity for a cutting garden. Even a small city apartment can provide a home for a few pots of flowers. If sunlight is insufficient, fluorescent lights can be rigged up to illuminate the plants. City gardeners can use windowsill space to start seeds of annuals early; even outdoor sills are suitable when they are warmed by the steam heat that escapes from poorly fitted window panes.

The first thing cut-flower lovers do when they move to a new home is turn over soil for a cutting garden, for flowers not only to grace the table but also to send back with weekend guests as favored remembrances.

Keep in mind that cutting gardens are not bound by the rules that govern most formal garden designs. Here the catchword is utility; you will want to arrange the plants to allow easy access for gathering flowers and replanting succession crops throughout the season. Cutting gardens can also become experiments in design; an accidental contrast of colors—perhaps a hot combination that breaks all the rules about harmonious colors—might inspire a great arrangement for next year's formal garden plan.

In the cutting garden, anything goes. Here's a place to mix the brightest cosmos cultivars with the hottest-colored cockscombs *(Celosia cristata)*. To make harvesting easy, plant gladiolus and other bulbs in neat rows. Dahlias can be grouped together by color or flower structure.

Remember to allow space for successive plantings of annuals like poppies or bulbous plants like gladiolus, in order to have flowers over a longer period. There should also be room for some of the weedier flowers, such as wild Queen Anne's lace *(Daucus carota* var. *carota)*, that look out of place in formal settings but terrific in an antique pottery vase.

Climbing flowers such as sweet peas *(Lathyrus odoratus)*, which need a trellis of string or netting to ramble over, present a charming rustic appearance that often works best in the informal surroundings of the cutting garden.

While the layout of your cutting garden will probably change from year to year, taller plants should always be at the rear, with the shorter plants up front. Be sure to allow room for plenty of narrow but workable pathways.

As always, soil should be well worked and reasonably fertile, but remember that with annuals, too much fertilizer often leads to fewer flowers.

A garden of annuals for cutting includes pink sweet peas, red nasturtiums, white marguerite daisies (grown as annuals in northern gardens), and perennial lavender and coreopsis.

Cutting Flowers

When cutting fresh flowers for the table or the house, make it an enjoyable outdoor activity that continues to bring pleasure indoors.

First, cut flowers in the early morning. Take along a bucket or pail of cool or tepid water, especially if you are gathering more than you need for just one or two bouquets. Choose flowers that are just about to or have recently opened. Use a sharp pair of scissors and cut the stems on a slant. There is nothing magical about that slanted cut—it merely opens more stem area to absorbing water. Put the flowers in the water as you cut them, and keep the bucket out of the sun.

Back in the kitchen, remove most of the leaves from the stems—they will quickly rot and cloud the water. Keep the flowers in the bucket of water in a cool place out of direct light for several hours to acclimate them to their indoor setting and extend the vase life. Some experts recommend a second cut, this time underwater, but if you put the flowers in water as soon as you cut them, the second cut is not necessary.

Always use a clean container to arrange flowers, and change the water every day if possible, using tepid water to prevent shock to the flowers. Fresh water every day, and perhaps the addition of a cut-flower preservative, is the best way to get the maximum life from cut flowers. Common practices, such as adding raw sugar, pennies, or diet soda to the water, do nothing except promote the growth of bacteria. The University of California did conduct an experiment in which a lemon-lime soft drink was added to water (one part soft drink to two parts of clean water), and tests did show that flowers lasted far longer than in plain water. Try this approach if you're so inclined.

Annuals for Cutting

When cutting flowers for an arrangement, try to include a mix of shapes and sizes—spiky and round flowers, larger and smaller flowers, and delicate blossoms to use as fillers in the bouquet. Don't overlook foliage—adding a few leaves to an arrangement can set off the flower colors. Here are some good annuals for cutting:

Spiky and vertical flowers: bells-of-Ireland, plume-type celosia, hollyhock, larkspur, salvia, and snapdragon.

Round flowers: bachelor's-button, blue lace flower, calendula, California poppy, China aster (shown in photo), coreopsis, cosmos, dianthus, geranium, gerbera, globe amaranth, love-in-a-mist, marigold, petunia, poppy, scabiosa, tassel flower, verbena, and zinnia.

Fillers: ageratum, animated oats (Avena spp.), baby's-breath, English daisy (Bellis perennis), feverfew, forget-me-not, quaking grass (Briza spp.), and sweet alyssum.

Other good annuals for cutting include spider flower, fragrant heliotrope, and sweet pea.

Allow space between groups of plants in a cutting garden so that you have easy access to the flowers. This garden includes zinnias, salvia, geraniums, and other long-stemmed blossoms good for cutting.

When you go out to the garden to cut flowers, take a bucket of cool water along with you and place the stems in the water as soon as you cut them.

Drying Flowers

*I*t's not necessary to say farewell to all your garden flowers at season's end. There are at least five ways to preserve their beauty to brighten up the dull days of winter.

Many blossoms, such as strawflowers *(Helichrysum bracteatum)*, most daisies, celosia, baby's-breath *(Gypsophila elegans)*, statice *(Limonium sinuatum)*, and the annual ornamental grasses, can be air-dried in a number of ways. Whatever the species, first remove all the leaves, then find a room or area that is reasonably dark but has plenty of ventilation.

Flowers with stiff stems, such as bells-of-Ireland *(Moluccella laevis)*, can simply be placed in a glass jar or vase until they are dry. Those that perch on floppy stems can be hung upside down in loose bundles from individual nails or hooks, or a number of bunches can be attached to wire clothes hangers. Or you can staple a big square of chicken wire to a wooden frame, and suspend the flowers with the stems hanging through the holes. The photographs below and on the opposite page show methods of drying flowers.

Often when a vase of flowers is forgotten for weeks, the owner will suddenly find the water has long gone but the flowers have dried naturally. This method works especially well for drying leaves.

Almost everyone has found a pressed flower or a four-leaf clover that somebody placed between the pages of a book and then forgot. Years, sometimes

Many annuals can be air-dried by gathering them in bunches and hanging them upside down in a well-ventilated place.

1 The classic way to dry flowers is to gather them in small bunches and hang them upside down in a dry, airy place out of direct sun. You might try suspending the flowers from coat hangers.

2 Many-petaled flowers such as zinnias and marigolds often dry best in a desiccant powder like silica gel. Lay the flower heads on a layer of desiccant, then sprinkle more powder over the flowers to cover.

Annuals for Drying

Many annuals are beautiful when dried. Among the best flowers for drying are holly-hock blossoms, zinnias, and cosmos dried in sand or silica gel; love-lies-bleeding, prince's-feather (Amaranthus hybridus *var.* erythrostachys), *cockscomb, and plumed celosia hung upside down and air-dried; and snapdragons dried in silica gel. Bells-of-Ireland should be hung to dry one stalk at a time. Most of the ornamental grasses, including hare's-tail grass* (Lagurus ovatus), *quaking grass* (Briza maxima *and B. minor*), *foxtail millet* (Setaria italica), *and squirreltail grass* (Hordeum jubatum) *dry perfectly by hanging bunches upside down in a dry room, but they must be picked when fresh. Don't forget the leaves of dusty-millers, which are elegant when pressed and dried.*

centuries later the flower falls out full of memories of another time. You can press flowers in an old telephone directory, alternating pages and flowers, then putting some bricks on top. Or use a heavy book and place the flowers between sheets of blotting paper to avoid staining the pages. Instead of using a book, you can buy a flower press or make one from a pair of wooden boards with holes drilled at each corner. Place the flowers between pieces of blotting paper or a few pages from a newspaper, then stack the layers between the boards. Tighten the boards with screws and wing nuts. The time required for drying varies between two and three weeks.

Another good method for drying flowers employs the fine white sand that is sold at building and home centers and used for filling children's sandboxes. First find a strong plastic or wooden box that can withstand the weight of the sand, then spread an inch-deep layer of sand on the bottom. Carefully place the flowers on that base and slowly sprinkle dry sand over and about the flowers until they are completely covered. Do not cover the container. Check after three weeks have passed to see if the flowers are dry.

Another way to dry flowers is to use silica gel. This is a drying agent that absorbs the moisture from flower petals in a very short time, working so quickly that frequently the floral colors are almost as fresh and bright as they were in life. Most craft shops carry silica gel. Although expensive, it can be dried and used again and again. Follow the instructions on the package.

Pest and Disease Control

*F*or plants, good hygiene is the best way to prevent disease. Never allow diseased or decaying plant material to lie about in the garden. You should even remove spent blossoms or dried leaves that have fallen naturally. When plants are given conditions to their liking and not grown under stress, they are able to withstand pests and diseases that would quickly kill their weaker cousins.

Take advantage of periodic walks through the garden to check out the health of your plants, so you can spot trouble in the early stages and take prompt action. Don't wait until a fatal disease or pest has ransacked the garden and destroyed your plants.

Slugs are major pests in many gardens. They are snails that have forsaken their shells in order to live a life gliding about at night on trails of slime, so they can chew holes in almost any plant material without being observed. Poisoned baits are effective, but avoid them if you have pets or small children. Instead, go out at night with a flashlight and sprinkle a few grains of salt on the tender bodies of the slugs. The salt quickly does them in without harming the garden. Or pick them up (wearing gloves!) and drop them into a can of soapy or salty water.

Beer traps—small pans of stale beer sunk into the ground—are a classic lure for slugs. Slugs do indeed seem to find beer irresistible, so much so that they inevitably fall into the traps and drown, but you may discover the traps so attractive that slugs come from all over the neighborhood to join the party. You may end up with even more slugs than you had before. Hand-picking and salt are better ways to kill slugs.

Insects like aphids, whiteflies, mealybugs, scale, and spider mites like to gather on the tender young growth at the tips of stems, in leaf axils (where leaves join the stem), and on the undersides of leaves. These pests can be controlled with applications of insecticidal soaps. But before you even look for the soap, see how many insects you can dislodge by aiming the water spray from a hose directly at the plants. After using the soap, check the plants every day. It often takes several applications of insecticidal soap to get rid of all the pests. Repeat the soap as many days as necessary until you see no further evidence of the pests.

Larger pests like caterpillars and Japanese beetles can be removed by hand, or you can use a product that lures insects with sex pheromones, attracting the victims to a disposable trap instead of a mate. If you opt for traps, place them outside the garden—traps tend to entice the pests right to your plants.

Insects like flea beetles and aphids can be controlled with applications of pyrethrum, an insecticide derived from the dried flower heads of the pyrethrum daisy *(Tanacetum coccineum)*. Remember that the action of light tends to break these products down chemically, often within a few hours after application; to prolong the action of pyrethrum apply it in late afternoon.

Rotenone is another plant-based insecticide manufactured from, among others, the roots of the tuba root *(Derris elliptica)*. Rotenone can cause lung irritation if inhaled, so use care in application. Botanical insecticides are effective but are best used as a last resort, since they kill beneficial insects as well as pests.

Be cautious when handling any pesticide. Even organic products are quite toxic when applied; their chief value is that they break down quickly and do not linger in the environment as do most synthetic or petroleum-based pesticides. Follow the directions on the label, and always wear gloves when applying any insecticidal sprays or dusts to plants. Be sure to store these materials correctly, too—by all means keep them out of reach of children.

Summer's End

Saving Seeds

Saving seeds of most hybrid annuals is a thankless task because not all of next year's flowers will be up to the standards of this year's cultivars; each year they will either get smaller in size or lose much of their color, or both. And it's impossible to tell which seedlings will be acceptable until they bloom (although some cultivars such as Nicotiana *'Lime Green' will flower true to type).*

Most of the annual seeds can be gathered, placed in paper envelopes, carefully labeled, then stored in a cool, dry, dark place until they are needed the following spring.

All the annual ornamental grasses are perfect for seed saving, as well as bishop's weed, winged everlasting, borage, creeping zinnia, tithonia, Johnny-jump-up, bells-of-Ireland, most tree mallows, California poppy, and starflower.

The end of summer is the time to watch for ripening seedpods to be dried for winter bouquets. It's the time of the year when flowers seem to sense the approach of cool weather and often burst forth with a last round of bloom. The colors seem brighter against the sharp blue skies that appear as temperatures fall and the air trades that misty softness of summer for the crystalline clarity of autumn.

As the days grow shorter you will be surprised by the strength of some of your annuals. The leaves of the various strawflowers (many have their origins in Australia) may shrivel with the inceasing cold of autumn, but their stiff petals of bright orange, red, yellow, or white resist the advances of frost, continuing to glow in the morning sun of early fall. The flowers of the poppy may be gone, but the marvelous seedpods are still there. Fall brings out the glorious colors of the flowering cabbages and kales, plants that need the nip of frost not only to grow but also for their colored leaves to shine. Then there are the pansies; they'll bloom all winter in areas of the country where winters are mild, but will even persist in northern gardens until almost the end of the year, or until snows get too deep for casual walks to the garden. Sweet alyssum, too, will keep flowering far into fall.

This is the time of the year to think about moving some of the geraniums *(Pelargonium* spp.*)* into pots and taking them indoors to a sunny windowsill for winter bloom. Some annuals, such as bedding begonias or ageratums, can be dug up and placed in small pots, where they will continue to produce flowers until the very short days of December. Polka-dot plants *(Hypoestes phyllostochya)* are really tropical perennials and are easily moved to indoor pots for the winter. Even marigolds will fight the advancing seasons and bring a spot of gold to the living room.

Where winters are cold, tender bulbs must come out of the ground in fall to be stored indoors. Dig up dahlia tubers after the first frost has blackened their leaves. Cut off the stems a few inches above the circle of tubers, remove as much soil as you can, and let them dry for a few days. Then you can brush off the remaining soil. Sort the tubers according to flower color, and store them in paper bags or boxes in a cool, dry place until the following spring. Save gladiolus corms in the same manner, and don't forget to dig up the large black tubers of four-o'clocks *(Mirabilis jalapa),* as well as the thick rhizomes of all the cannas.

Older garden books advise pulling geraniums from the garden in fall, shaking off the dirt, and hanging them in a frost-free place for winter's duration. In spring the plants are cut back and replanted. You may want to try this method—sometimes it works and sometimes it doesn't. When you realize the savings that could be applied to other plants in the coming season, it may well be worth the effort.

If you have a greenhouse, a sunporch, or room in the basement for a light garden, you can take cuttings of many annuals to start new plants. Cut healthy stems about 3 to 5 inches long using a sharp, clean knife or razor blade, slicing just below the point where a leaf stalk joins the stem. Remove any damaged leaves and flowers, and neatly cut off any bottom leaves.

Fill a seed flat or some pots with dampened sterile soil or a potting mix. Tamp it down, then make a hole with a pencil to three-quarters of the pot's depth. Insert the cutting, making sure that the base of the stem is in contact with the dirt at the bottom. Then firm the soil around the stem. Put the potted plant in a plastic bag with the opening at the top. Seal the bag

Summer's End CONTINUED

1 As summer ends, you can take cuttings of geraniums and other annuals to root for winter houseplants. First clip off the flower heads.

2 Next, select healthy shoots to use as cuttings. Young, vigorous growing tips or side shoots make the best cuttings for indoor plants.

1 Coleus makes a colorful houseplant. In late winter you can take cuttings from the indoor plants and root them to have new plants for the garden.

2 Coleus cuttings root quickly in water. Strip off the lower leaves, and insert the stems into water. Change the water once or twice a week so that bacteria won't build up.

3 Remove the leaves from the bottom third or half of each cutting, as shown here. Have pots full of moist potting mix ready for planting the cuttings.

4 Dip the end of each cutting in rooting hormone powder if you like (they will also root without it), and insert each into the potting mix almost up to the lowest leaves.

3 In a matter of weeks the coleus cuttings will develop good roots. Once you get a good assortment, you can plant the cuttings in pots.

4 Plant the rooted cuttings in a light, porous but moisture-retentive potting mix. Handle them carefully during planting to avoid injuring the delicate roots.

EARTH·WISE
TIP

One of the jobs that is best left until the cool days of autumn is scrubbing clay pots, then carefully storing them for another season. Don't forget to wash the plastic pots too. Unless they are severely broken or brittle, most plastic pots can be used for more than one season. Your local nursery may even give credit for returned pots.

Summer's End CONTINUED

After you've pulled up the dead annuals and added them to the compost, along with gathered leaves, twigs, and the rest of the horticultural rubbish, give the soil a final rake. Then mulch the open soil, either with an additional layer of shredded leaves or perhaps a bushel or two of pine needles. You'll find the neat and orderly look of the mulch will just contribute to the look of the winter garden. Till it in spring to add organic matter.

In fall, pull and compost annuals as they stop blooming or are killed by frost, remove stakes and supports, and clean up the garden before winter sets in.

with a twist of wire to create a tiny greenhouse. Put the container in bright light but not direct sun.

Keep the soil moist but never soggy. In about two to three weeks, give the cutting a slight tug to check if rooting has commenced. If it hasn't, pull out the cutting to see if the end has started to rot. If everything looks healthy, try again, but make doubly sure that the stem bottom is in contact with the soil; it needs this stimulus to start new roots. You may wish to dip the end of the cutting in rooting hormone powder as well.

You can also root cuttings of some annuals in a glass of water. Impatiens, coleus, begonias, and geraniums will soon begin to produce roots. After a num-

1 *Hollyhocks (shown here) overwinter and bloom again a second year in many gardens, so cut back the stems to a few inches from the ground.*

2 *When the soil begins to freeze, mulch the plants well to prevent the roots from heaving during alternating freezes and thaws in winter.*

ber of roots begin to appear, start adding small amounts of sand or soil to the water every few days. That way you won't have a tangled mass of roots to sort out when it's time to transplant, and the soil or sand will stimulate the roots to grow new root hairs, which are the true movers of food and water to the plants.

After saving as many annuals as you can and safely storing the bulbs and tubers for the coming spring, there is still cleanup work in the garden.

Perhaps you have collected some bushel baskets or plastic trash bags that are full of leaves that fell from your or your neighbor's trees. After shredding, either add them to that compost heap or, using a small cultivator, mix them into the garden soil so that they can decay over the winter and grace the soil for spring.

Before the temperatures really plummet, pull out all the dead plants, carefully shake off all the dirt you can, and move them to the compost heap. At the same time, take care of those late-growing weeds. Then carefully rake the soil, and neaten up the edges.

Clean the dirt off your garden tools. Wind up the garden twine, and wash your garden gloves. Clean and coil the hoses, and collect all those labels that now dot the garden. Then go indoors, make a good cup of tea or coffee, gather your new seed catalogues, and get ready for the wonderful year ahead.

Regional Calendar of Garden Care

 Spring

✿ *Summer*

COOL CLIMATES

Spring

- In early spring, start seeds indoors for slow-to-bloom plants like begonias.

- As soon as soil thaws, dig or till as needed to prepare for planting cold-tolerant annuals. Plant seeds of hardy annuals when soil is ready.

- Start a new compost heap and turn it regularly. Begin to work aged compost into soil.

- Prepare soil for planting tender annuals.

- When all danger of frost is past and soil has warmed, direct sow or transplant tender annuals outdoors (use transplants in zones 5 and north).

- As annuals begin to grow, pinch back plants for bushier growth and better flowering.

- In late spring, begin weeding and watching for pests.

Summer

- In early summer, plant fast-growing annuals for a second crop of flowers.

- Deadhead, weed, and water as needed. Keep watching for pests, and take action at the first sign of trouble.

- Remember to mulch the garden.

- Check local garden centers and nurseries for annuals on sale. Check sale plants carefully before buying.

- Start collecting flowers for drying.

- Start a garden diary and rate annuals that perform well for inclusion in next year's garden.

- Visit local botanical gardens to see display annuals and gather ideas for next year's garden.

WARM CLIMATES

Spring

- Sow annuals to hide the ripening leaves of spring bulbs.

- Pinch annuals as they grow for better flowering.

- When danger of frost is past, plant tender annuals outdoors.

- In late spring, plant a second crop of early-blooming annuals.

- Check garden centers and nurseries for annuals on sale. Check sale plants carefully before buying.

- Mulch the garden. Weed, water, and deadhead as needed. Watch for pests and take action at the first sign of trouble.

- Pinch annuals as they grow for bushier plants and better flowering.

Summer

- Plant a second crop of late-blooming annuals for continued color in the garden.

- Remember to fertilize annuals in containers and make sure they have plenty of water.

- Keep deadheading flowers for continued bloom unless you want to save seeds.

- Start collecting flowers for drying.

- Start a garden diary and rate annuals' performance; include the best in next year's garden.

- Visit local botanical gardens to see display annuals and gather ideas for next year's garden.

Fall

- Collect seeds of species and cultivars that will breed true to type.
- Take cuttings of impatiens, begonias, coleus, and geraniums to root for winter houseplants.
- Dig and pot up marigolds for a few more weeks of bloom indoors.
- At night, use spunbonded polyester covers to protect late-blooming annuals from early frosts. Remove covers during the day.
- Remember to keep turning compost heaps.
- Have your soil tested.
- Start sending for seed catalogues. Join plant societies that offer seed exchanges.
- Clean up any weeds, frost-damaged plants, and faded flowers in the garden. Clean and store tools. Turn off outdoor water taps.

- Plant seeds of cold-hardy annuals for extended winter bloom.
- Gather seeds of species and cultivars that will breed true to type.
- Take cuttings of impatiens, begonias, coleus, and geraniums to root for winter houseplants.
- At night, use spunbonded polyester covers to protect late-blooming annuals from early frosts. Remove covers during the day.
- Continue to weed, water, fertilize, and watch for pests.
- Remember to turn compost heaps.
- Start sending for seed catalogues.

 Winter

- Plan next year's annual garden. Order seeds early for the best selection.
- When seeds arrive, separate the packets into groups according to their growing needs. You might have one group to start early indoors, a group to direct-sow as soon as garden soil is workable, and a group of fast-growing plants to sow outdoors when frost danger is past.
- In late winter, start slow-blooming annuals on windowsills or under lights. Start geraniums (*Pelargonium* spp.*) in February for June flowers.
- Turn compost heaps when they are not frozen.
- Wash and sterilize clay and plastic pots for reuse next spring.
- Save wood ashes for the garden.
- In late winter, start attending local and regional flower shows.

- Weed, water, deadhead, and fertilize annuals blooming in winter gardens.
- Have your soil tested.
- Plan next year's garden. Order seeds early for best selection.
- In late winter, start seeds for slow-to-bloom plants like begonias. For geraniums in early May, start seeds in late December.
- As soon as soil thaws, dig or till as needed. Plant pansies in the garden as soon as soil is workable.
- Start a new compost heap and remember to turn it regularly. Begin to work aged compost into the soil.
- Wash and sterilize clay and plastic pots for reuse in spring.
- Start attending regional flower shows.

This table offers a basic outline of garden care by season. The tasks for each season differ for warm and cool climates: warm climates correspond to USDA Plant Hardiness zones 8 through 11, and cool climates to zones 2 through 7. Obviously, there are substantial climate differences within these broad regions. Be sure to study local factors affecting the microclimate of your garden, such as elevation and proximity of water.

Annuals for American Gardens

*T*his section provides concise information on more than 150 plants recommended for annual gardens. The plants have been selected on the basis of beauty, adaptability, and availability. If you're looking for plants for particular uses—of a certain height, for instance, or with flowers of a certain color—look first at the Color Range and Growth Habit columns. If you need plants for a shady spot, look at the Growing Conditions column. Or look at the photos, read the descriptions, and then decide which plants will grow well in your garden.

About Plant Names

Plants appear in alphabetical order by the genus name, shown in bold type. On the next line is the most widely used common name. The third line contains the complete botanical name: genus, species, and where applicable, a variety or cultivar name.

Common names vary, but botanical names are the same everywhere. If you learn botanical names, you'll always get the plant you want from a mail-order nursery or local garden center. One gardener's Dahlberg daisy may be another gardener's goldenfleece, but both gardeners will recognize the plant if they know its scientific name: *Dyssodia tenuiloba*.

When several species in a genus are similar in appearance and cultural needs, they are listed together in a single entry in the chart. In the case of a genus containing two or more vastly different species that cannot be covered in a single entry, each of the recommended species is given a separate entry in the chart.

The second column of the chart provides a brief plant description. Look here to see if the plant is vertical, bushy, low, or vining.

Color Range

The color dots following each description indicate the color *family*, and are not a literal rendering of the flower color. A plant given a pink dot might be pale blush pink, clear pink, or bright rose pink.

Time of Bloom

Bloom time is given by season and may vary from one region to another according to climate, weather, and growing conditions. For example, sweet peas *(Lathyrus odoratus)* bloom in late spring and early summer in northern gardens, but can be grown for winter flowers in warm climates. During a cold year when spring comes late, tender plants should go into the garden later and will thus bloom later.

If you want more specific information on when a plant flowers in your area, ask your local USDA county cooperative extension office.

Hardiness

Plant hardiness is generally an indication of the coldest temperatures a plant is likely to survive. But many plants also have limits to the amount of heat they can tolerate. In this chart hardiness is expressed by three categories generally used to describe the temperature needs of plants grown as annuals: hardy, half-hardy, and tender. Hardy annuals can tolerate the most cold, and tender annuals the least. All three categories are described in detail on pages 6–9. If you are looking for annuals to plant for bloom in cool or warm weather, see page 127 for a listing of annuals by hardiness category.

Growing Conditions

The last column of the chart summarizes the best growing conditions for the plant including its light, moisture, and soil requirements.

			Flower Color	Time of Bloom	Growth Habit	Hardiness	Growing Conditions
	ABELMOSCHUS MUSK MALLOW *Abelmoschus moschatus*	A tender perennial grown as an annual. Bushy shoots bear 3- to 4-in., yellow to red hibiscus-like flowers with contrasting centers. Broad leaves have 5–7 deep lobes. Seeds have musky aroma. Plants are sometimes listed as Hibiscus abelmoschus.		Early summer to frost	Height: 2–6' Spacing: 1–1½'	Half-hardy	Full sun to light shade. Well-drained soil with average moisture. Plants grow best in zone 6 and warmer; start seeds indoors and transplant when danger of frost has passed. Plants can be dug in autumn and grown as an indoor container plant.
	ABUTILON FLOWERING MAPLE, CHINESE-LANTERN *Abutilon hybridum*	A tender soft-wooded perennial shrub often grown as a houseplant or annual. It has broad, sometimes variegated, maplelike leaves and solitary, nodding, 2-in., hollyhock-like flowers in shades of white, red, yellow, and peach.		Summer to autumn	Height: 1–3' Spacing: 1–3'	Tender	Full sun to partial shade; grows best with afternoon shade in zones 7–10. Average garden soil. Start seeds indoors in midwinter and transplant seedlings outdoors after all danger of frost has passed. Plants are perennial in zones 9–11.
	AGERATUM FLOSSFLOWER *Ageratum houstonianum*	A longtime favorite for edging and borders. Numerous clusters of ¼-in., feathery, light blue flower heads appear above mounds of small, velvety leaves. Lavender- or white-flowered cultivars are available.		Early summer to autumn	Height: 6–18" Spacing: 6–12"	Tender	Full sun to partial shade, with afternoon shade in zones 7–10. Average, well-drained soil. Start seeds indoors in midwinter and transplant seedlings outdoors after all danger of frost has passed. Deadhead for continued bloom.
	AGROSTEMMA CORN COCKLE *Agrostemma githago*	Showy magenta, 1- to 2-in., 5-petaled flowers atop slender stems. The petals are delicately etched with darker stripes and a few dark spots. Pairs of narrow, lance-shaped, downy leaves clasp the stem. The dark seeds are poisonous.		Late spring to early autumn	Height: 1–2' Spacing: 6–12"	Half-hardy	Full sun. Well-drained soil of low fertility. Sow seeds either in early spring or late autumn, and thin seedlings to 6–12 in. apart. Provide support if plants become droopy and deadhead to prolong flowering season.
	ALCEA HOLLYHOCK *Alcea rosea*	An old-fashioned biennial with tall stems bearing a spike of 2- to 4-in., single or double flowers in purple, red, pink, white, or yellow. The 5 petals have a crepelike texture. Plant may be listed by its old name, Althaea.		Summer to early autumn	Height: 4–8' Spacing: 1–1½'	Very Hardy	Full sun. Well-drained garden soil rich in humus. Plant seeds ¼–⅓ in. deep in the desired location. This biennial will flower the second year and usually self-seeds thereafter. Some varieties may bloom the first season if started indoors.

Annuals for American Gardens

			Flower Color	Time of Bloom	Growth Habit	Hardiness	Growing Conditions
	AMARANTHUS LOVE-LIES-BLEEDING, TASSEL FLOWER *Amaranthus caudatus*	A striking plant. Dense chenillelike clusters of tiny bright red, pink, or white flowers festoon the branches. The long-lasting flower tassels can be used in fresh or dried arrangements. Varieties with various foliage colors are available.	●	Summer to early autumn	Height: 1–3' Spacing: 9–15"	Tender	Full sun. Well-drained soil with low fertility. Seeds need warmth to germinate. In zone 8 or warmer, sow seeds where desired in early spring. In colder regions start indoors and transplant seedlings after last frost.
	AMARANTHUS JOSEPH'S-COAT, TAMPALA *Amaranthus tricolor*	An annual grown more for its brilliant, multicolored foliage than for the minute clusters of flowers borne in the axils of its leaves. This bold plant has 2- to 4-in. green leaves with bright blotches of yellow and red (or sometimes purple).		Late spring to autumn	Height: 1–4' Spacing: 1–2'	Tender	Full sun. For best foliage color, grow in well-drained, relatively nutrient-poor soil. Cultural requirements are identical to those of A. caudatus.
	AMMOBIUM WINGED EVERLASTING *Ammobium alatum*	A tender perennial named for the winged ridges that run along its stems. Long-lasting, solitary, 1½-in., daisylike flower heads have yellow centers surrounded by chaffy white bracts. Leaves are covered with woolly white hairs.	○	Late spring to late summer	Height: 2–3' Spacing: 8–15"	Tender	Full sun. Sandy soil with average moisture. In zones 7 and colder, start seeds indoors and transplant when danger of frost has passed. These easily grown plants self-seed in zones 7 and warmer. Ammobium grows as a perennial in zones 10–11.
	ANAGALLIS BLUE PIMPERNEL *Anagallis monelli*	A tender perennial related to the scarlet pimpernel. Plants bear 5-lobed, ¾-in., blue or purple flowers with white, starlike centers. Stems are clad in narrow, 1-in. leaves.	○●●●	Summer	Height: 8–18" Spacing: 1–1½'	Tender	Full sun to very light shade. Average garden soil conditions. Plants grow best in warm weather. Start seeds indoors in early spring and transplant seedlings outdoors after the last frost. Grow as a perennial in zones 9–11, as an annual elsewhere.
	ANTIRRHINUM SNAPDRAGON *Antirrhinum majus*	A familiar item in florist shops. Sprawling stems bear abundant terminal clusters of 1½-in., pouched flowers with a 2-lobed upper lip and 3-lobed lower lip. Colors range from white to yellow, orange, red, and purple.	○●○●●●	Late spring to frost	Height: 2–3' Spacing: 6–12"	Very Hardy	Full sun to partial shade; provide afternoon shade in zones 8–11. Well-drained, evenly moist soil. Plant seeds by sprinkling them on the soil; they need light to germinate. Start indoors 6–8 weeks before planting in zones 4 and colder.

			Flower Color	Time of Bloom	Growth Habit	Hardiness	Growing Conditions
	ARCTOTIS AFRICAN DAISY *Arctotis stoechadifolia*	An annual available in an astounding range of flower colors. The classic version has 3-in., daisylike flowers whose white petals have a lavender band at their bases and violet centers. The undersides of the petals are light lavender.	◯ ● ● ● ●	Summer to frost	Height: 2–3' Spacing: 8–12"	Half-hardy	Full sun. Average garden soil conditions. Start indoors in late winter in zone 6 and colder; elsewhere, when soil is warm, sow ¼ in. deep where plants are desired. Deadheading or frequent cutting prolongs bloom. Arctotis is an excellent cut flower.
	ARGEMONE PRICKLY POPPY *Argemone mexicana*	A drought-tolerant annual with attractive, blue-green, spiny foliage variegated with white. Leaves provide stark contrast for large (2- to 2½-in.), fragile, sweetly scented flowers that range in color from lemon yellow to light orange. Sap is bright yellow.	●	Early summer to autumn	Height: 1–3' Spacing: 1–2'	Half-hardy	Full sun. Well-drained soil. Prickly poppy grows particularly well in hot climates. Sow seeds ⅛ in. deep in mid-spring where plants are desired. Deadhead to prolong flowering season.
	ASCLEPIAS BLOODFLOWER *Asclepias curassavica*	Showy clusters of ornate scarlet and orange flowers, blooming at the tips and in the axils of sturdy branches. Pairs of 5-in., narrow, lance-shaped leaves are deep green and nearly clasp the stems. Plants produce attractive 4-in. pod fruits.	● ●	Summer to frost	Height: 2–3' Spacing: 1–2'	Tender	Full sun. Very moist soil. A tender, tropical perennial in zones 10–11; elsewhere grow it as an annual. Start indoors in midwinter and transplant outdoors after frost. Dig in autumn and grow indoors as a houseplant.
	BEGONIA WAX BEGONIA *Begonia × semperflorens-cultorum*	A tender perennial used as a bedding annual. Mounds of semisucculent, broad, deep green or bronze leaves accent loose clusters of white, pink, or red flowers with slightly irregular petals. Available in single- or double-flowered forms.	◯ ● ●	Summer to early autumn	Height: 8–12" Spacing: 8–12"	Tender	Full sun to light shade; needs afternoon shade in zones 7–11. Moist soil rich in humus. Start seeds indoors 4–5 months before last frost. Wax begonia makes an excellent indoor container plant.
	BORAGO BORAGE *Borago officinalis*	A favorite since classical times for its clusters of ¾-in., violet-blue flowers that look like 5-pointed stars with protruding stamens. Its bristly leaves smell like cucumbers. Flowers and leaves are edible. Borage is a good plant for attracting bees.	● ●	Early summer to frost	Height: 1–2' Spacing: 1–1½'	Hardy	Full sun to light shade; needs afternoon shade in zones 8–11. Average, well-drained soil. For continuous bloom sow seeds where desired at monthly intervals. Deadhead withering flowers to prolong bloom. Borage does not transplant well.

Annuals for American Gardens

		Flower Color	Time of Bloom	Growth Habit	Hardiness	Growing Conditions
BRACHYCOME SWAN RIVER DAISY *Brachycome iberidifolia*	An excellent cut flower with abundant single, 1-in., daisy-like heads with blue, pink, rose, or white petals surrounding golden centers. Deeply cut leaves are scattered on long stems. Plants are good for filling borders or edges.	○ ◉ ◉ ●	*Summer to early autumn*	Height: 9–18" Spacing: 1–1½'	Tender	*Full sun. Soils with average moisture and fertility. Start plants indoors. Sow seeds ¼ in. deep 5 weeks before last frost and transplant to desired locations. Successive late spring plantings prolong the short flowering period into autumn.*
BRASSICA KALE, ORNAMENTAL KALE *Brassica oleracea* Acephala group	Ornamental relative of the familiar vegetable. This plant is a biennial grown for its rosettes of leaves that range in color from white to deep lavender blue to green variegated with white, red, or purple. Leaf margins are wavy to crispy.		*Late summer to winter*	Height: 8–12" Spacing: 8–12"	Very Hardy	*Full sun. Soil with ample moisture and good drainage. Ornamental kale grows best in cool weather, and colors improve with frost. Plant seeds in summer where desired. Protect from caterpillars of the cabbage butterfly.*
BRIZA QUAKING GRASS *Briza maxima*	A decorative grass whose dangling 2- to 3-in. panicles of bright green, heart-shaped flowers rise above the foliage and turn tan in the summer. Lush, soft, 6-in. leaves are ¼ in. wide. Dried fruit heads can be used in arrangements.	◉	*Late spring to early summer*	Height: 1–2' Spacing: 2–4"	Hardy	*Full sun. Fertile soil. Provide ample moisture, especially while the grass is starting to grow rapidly; thereafter, it is more drought tolerant. Sow as for grass seed in early to mid-spring. Plants usually self-sow thereafter.*
BROWALLIA BUSH VIOLET *Browallia speciosa*	A bushy plant bearing 2-in., tubular, 5-petaled, violet-blue (or sometimes white) flowers. The bright green leaves are lance shaped and scattered along the stems. Browallias are good cut flowers and look attractive in hanging baskets.	○ ● ●	*Summer*	Height: 1–2' Spacing: 1–1½'	Tender	*Partial to full shade. Moist, but not wet, soil. This tender perennial is grown as an annual except in zones 10–11. Start seeds indoors 6–8 weeks before last frost; then transplant. Plants make excellent houseplants if potted before frost.*
CALADIUM ELEPHANT'S-EAR, FANCY-LEAVED CALADIUM *Caladium × hortulanum*	A tropical perennial grown as an annual for its foliage rather than for the small, hidden flowers. Cultivars come in a wide range of leaf colors (green, white, salmon, red, or variegated) and shapes (heart, lance, triangular, or arrow).		*Leaves produced from frost to frost*	Height: 2½–3½' Spacing: 1½–2½'	Tender	*Partial to full shade. Moist, well-drained soil rich in humus. Propagate by division of small tubers in the autumn. Store over winter (or continue growing indoors as a container plant), and replant outside after the last frost.*

			Flower Color	Time of Bloom	Growth Habit	Hardiness	Growing Conditions
	CALCEOLARIA POCKETBOOK PLANT *Calceolaria integrifolia*	A bushy, tender evergreen perennial that can be grown as an annual. Clusters of ⅓- to ½-in. flowers have fused petals that form a pouch. Petals are usually yellow or dark red with contrasting mottled spots. Calceolarias are good houseplants.	● ●	Early summer to frost	Height: 3–4' Spacing: 1½–2½'	Half-hardy	Partial to full shade. Moist, well-drained, slightly acidic soil. Start seeds indoors 3 months before last frost. Press seeds lightly into soil surface and provide moisture as seedlings develop. Plants also can be propagated by cuttings.
	CALENDULA POT MARIGOLD *Calendula officinalis*	An old-fashioned annual whose cheery flowers can be used as a culinary herb. Marigold-like, 2- to 4-in. flowers come in colors ranging from cream to yellow to orange and are excellent for cutting. Pale green leaves are pungent.	●	Late spring to autumn or winter in warm climates	Height: 1–2' Spacing: 1–1½'	Hardy	Full sun to light shade. Average, well-drained soil. Calendulas are very easy to grow even in poor soil if sufficient water is supplied. Plant seeds where desired in fall or early spring. Deadhead to prolong flowering.
	CALLISTEPHUS CHINA ASTER *Callistephus chinensis*	A plant of the daisy family that comes in an astounding variety of flower and plant forms. All have showy, solitary, asterlike flowers on relatively long stalks with toothed leaves. The blue, violet, or pink flowers are excellent for cutting.	○ ● ● ●	Summer to frost	Height: 8–24" Spacing: 1–1½'	Tender	Full sun. Average, well-drained soil. Plant directly where desired, or for earlier blooms start seeds indoors in late winter. To control susceptibility to wilt diseases, plant in a new location every year.
	CAMPANULA CANTERBURY-BELLS *Campanula medium*	Biennials and annuals that are longtime favorites for beds and borders. Bell-shaped, 1-in. flowers are blue, pink, rose, or white. Lance-shaped leaves have toothed edges. Double-flowered cultivars are available.	○ ● ● ●	Midspring to summer	Height: 2–4' Spacing: 8–15"	Hardy	Full sun. Moist, well-drained, humus-rich soil. Plant both biennial and annual cultivars in early spring. Both grow best in cool climates. Mulch biennials during winter.
	CANNA GARDEN CANNA *Canna × generalis*	Hybrids of tropical perennials grown as annuals for their large (4-in.), showy, irregular flowers, usually in shades ranging from red to yellow to pink or in variegated combinations. The lush, bold foliage is usually gray green.	● ○ ● ●	Summer	Height: 2–5' Spacing: 2–3'	Tender	Full sun. Moist, fertile soil rich in humus. Start seeds in winter by nicking them and planting them ½ in. deep in sandy soil. Or plant cuttings of last year's tubers in the spring after last frost. Dig up tubers before autumn frost.

Annuals for American Gardens

		Flower Color	Time of Bloom	Growth Habit	Hardiness	Growing Conditions
CAPSICUM ORNAMENTAL PEPPER *Capsicum annuum*	A bushy, tender perennial grown for its small (³/4-in.), bright red pepper fruits. The ½-in., white, 5-petaled flowers have 5 golden anthers clustered at the center. The leaves are evergreen. Ornamental pepper is an excellent container plant.	○	Summer	Height: 8–30" Spacing: 8–15"	Tender	Full sun. Moist, well-drained soil. Sow seeds indoors in late winter and transplant after last frost. Plants can be potted and moved indoors before first autumn frost.
CARDIO-SPERMUM BALLOON VINE, LOVE-IN-A-PUFF *Cardiospermum halica-cabum*	A creeping vine with tendrils extending from clusters of small (¼-in.) but numerous 4-petaled white flowers. The fruits, which resemble 1-in. green balloons, contain black, pea-sized seeds with a white, heart-shaped blotch.	○	Summer	Height: 10–12' Spacing: 3–5'	Tender	Full sun. Average soil conditions. *Cardiospermum* can be grown as a perennial in zones 9–11, as an annual elsewhere. Start indoors 6 weeks before last frost. In zones 8 and warmer, it self-seeds and may become weedy.
CASSIA PARTRIDGE PEA *Cassia fasciculata*	A native of the eastern U.S. bearing open, 1-in., bright yellow flowers with 10 dark brown, drooping anthers at their centers. Flowers are borne in the axils of compound leaves that move slightly when touched.		Early summer to mid-autumn	Height: 1–3' Spacing: 8–24"	Hardy	Full sun. Well-drained soil; prefers sandy loams. Plant seeds in the early spring where desired. Partridge pea often self-sows.
CATANANCHE CUPID'S-DART *Catananche caerulea*	Lavender-blue, daisylike flower heads with flat, toothed outer petals atop long stems. The gray-green, grassy foliage grows mostly in clumps at the bottom of the stems. White-flowered and white-and-blue-flowered cultivars are also available.	○ ◐ ◐	Late spring to late summer	Height: 1–2' Spacing: 1–1½'	Hardy	Full sun. Average soil. Start seeds indoors in early spring in zone 6 and colder. In zone 7 and warmer plant directly where desired. Plants also can be propagated from root-stock cuttings. Cupid's-dart is a perennial that usually flowers the first year.
CATHARANTHUS MADAGASCAR PERIWINKLE *Catharanthus roseus*	A plant that so closely resembles Vinca it is sometimes listed as V. roseus. However, this periwinkle has pink or white, 1½-in. flowers whose 5 flaring petals show a dark eye where they join together. An all-white cultivar is also available.	○ ◐	Late spring to autumn	Height: 1–2' Spacing: 1–2'	Tender	Full sun. Well-drained, moist soil of average fertility. Plants grow best in high heat and humidity. In regions colder than zone 10 start seeds indoors in late winter. *Catharanthus* is grown as an annual north of zone 9 and as a perennial in zones 9–11.

			Flower Color	Time of Bloom	Growth Habit	Hardiness	Growing Conditions
CELOSIA COCKSCOMB, WOOLFLOWER *Celosia cristata* Childsii group	A colorful annual grown for its elaborate crested flower heads. Minute flowers are usually brilliant red, orange, yellow, or gold. The tiny velvety flower heads appear in 6- to 12-in. masses resembling lumps of coral. Foliage is sometimes variegated.		● ●	Midsummer to frost	Height: 1–2' Spacing: 6–12"	Tender	Full sun to very light shade; prefers some afternoon shade in warm climates. Moist, even damp soil rich in humus.
CELOSIA PLUMED COCKSCOMB *Celosia cristata* Plumosa group	A colorful annual grown for its chaffy, feathery flower heads. Tiny flowers are clustered in 6- to 12-in. plumes, usually red, orange, or yellow. The pointed leaves are glossy green, sometimes variegated or purple.		● ●	Midsummer to frost	Height: 1–2¹/2' Spacing: 6–12"	Tender	Full sun to very light shade; prefers some afternoon shade in warm climates. Moist, even damp soil rich in humus.
CENTAUREA DUSTY-MILLER *Centaurea cineraria*	A compact perennial usually grown as an annual for its mounds of woolly, white foliage. The 1-in., purple or yellow, solitary flower heads resemble bachelor's-buttons. This is a good plant for seaside gardens.		○ ●	Summer	Height: 1–1¹/2' Spacing: 6–9"	Hardy	Full sun. Well-drained soil. Start seedlings indoors in late winter and transplant in spring. Do not overwater since plants are prone to damping-off fungus. Plants will grow as perennials in zone 5 and warmer.
CENTAUREA BACHELOR'S-BUTTON, CORNFLOWER *Centaurea cyanus*	A favorite annual for cutting gardens. The 1¹/2-in. flowers are usually clear blue but sometimes are pink, purple, or white. Single- and double-flowered cultivars are available as are dwarf forms. Foliage is gray green.		○ ○ ○ ● ●	Late spring to late summer	Height: 1–3' Spacing: 6–12"	Hardy	Full sun. Well-drained soil with average moisture. Plants grow best in cool weather. Sow this easy-to-grow annual in fall or early spring where plants are desired. In zone 3 and colder, start indoors in early spring and transplant as soon as soil can be worked.
CENTAUREA SWEET-SULTAN *Centaurea moschata*	A fast-growing annual whose fragrant, 2- to 3-in. flower heads look like large bachelor's-buttons. Flowers are yellow, rose pink, white, or purple. Lance-shaped, toothed, bright gray-green leaves are scattered along the branching stems.		○ ○ ●	Summer to early autumn	Height: 1–2' Spacing: 6–8"	Half-hardy	Full sun. Well-drained soil. Plants grow well in warm weather. Sow the seeds where plants are desired or, in zone 4 and colder, start indoors in early spring and plant outdoors in mid-spring.

Annuals for American Gardens

		Flower Color	Time of Bloom	Growth Habit	Hardiness	Growing Conditions
	CERINTHE HONEYWORT *Cerinthe major*	A "bee flower" that attracts insects with its abundant sweet nectar. The ³⁄₄-in. yellow flowers with purple tops hang down in loosely coiled clusters above the rough, clasping, elongated, heart-shaped leaves.	Summer	Height: 6–20" Spacing: 9–12"	Hardy	Full sun. Average, well-drained soil. Plants grow best in cool weather. Start seeds indoors in early spring and transplant seedlings after the last frost.
	CHRYSAN-THEMUM TRICOLOR CHRYSANTHEMUM *Chrysanthemum carinatum*	A bold annual chrysanthemum with daisylike flowers. The 2¹⁄₂-in. flower heads have bands of red, yellow, orange, white, or purple in various combinations surrounding violet centers. Dense, pungent foliage is light green and feathery.	Early to late summer	Height: 2–3' Spacing: 1–1¹⁄₂'	Hardy	Full sun to partial shade. Well-drained soil with average moisture conditions. Plants grow best when weather is cool and dry. Sow seeds outdoors in early spring where plants are desired.
	CIRSIUM RED THISTLE *Cirsium japonicum*	A short-lived, native Japanese perennial that flowers in the first year, like an annual. The 1- to 2-in. thistle flowers are deep magenta and bloom singly or in small clusters above the foliage. The prickly leaves have spiny edges.	Summer	Height: 2' Spacing: 1'	Hardy	Full sun to partial shade. Well-drained soil with abundant moisture. Sow seeds outdoors in early spring where plants are desired.
	CLARKIA FAREWELL-TO-SPRING, SATIN FLOWER *Clarkia amoena*	A Pacific Coast native that heralds the end of spring and the coming of summer. Showy, 2- to 4-in. flowers have 4 petals in pink, red, white, lavender, or combinations, often with darker colors at their bases.	Late spring to late summer	Height: 1¹⁄₂–2¹⁄₂' Spacing: 6–9"	Hardy	Full sun to light shade. Average, well-drained garden soil. Sow seeds outdoors in late autumn in zone 9 and warmer, or in early spring in zone 8 and colder. Plants are drought tolerant once flowering starts.
	CLEOME SPIDER FLOWER *Cleome hasslerana*	An annual grown for its airy pastel clouds of ornate flowers. Borne at the top of stiff stems with pungent, compound leaves, the 2- to 3-in. flowers have long, protruding stamens. The rose pink petals usually fade quickly.	Midsummer to early autumn	Height: 4–5' Spacing: 1'	Half-hardy	Full sun to partial shade. Well-drained soil that is on the dry side and without additional fertilizer. In zone 5 and warmer plant seeds outdoors in early spring; in zone 4 and colder start indoors in late winter.

			Flower Color	Time of Bloom	Growth Habit	Hardiness	Growing Conditions
	COBAEA CUP-AND-SAUCER VINE *Cobaea scandens*	A vine that climbs by tendrils and produces showy, 1- to 2½-in., violet and white cup-like flowers surrounded by a saucerlike green calyx. Gold stamens protrude from flower centers. A white-flowered form is available.	○ ●	Late spring to frost	Height: 10–25' Spacing: 1–2'	Tender	Full sun. Well-drained, sandy soil that is not too fertile. This fast-growing, long-flowering plant can be grown as a perennial in zone 9 and warmer. Elsewhere, grow as an annual, starting seeds indoors in late winter.
	COIX JOB'S TEARS *Coix lacryma-jobi*	An ornamental grass resembling corn, with flat, 1- to 2-ft. leaves and tassels of male flowers at tops of stems. Clusters of female flowers produce hard, ½-in., light gray, egg-shaped fruits.	○ ●	Summer	Height: 3–6' Spacing: 1'	Half-hardy	Full sun. Moist, well-drained soil. This evergreen grass can be grown as a perennial in zone 9 and warmer and as an annual elsewhere. Start seeds indoors in late winter and transplant in early to mid-spring.
	COLEUS COLEUS *Coleus × hybridus*	A frost-sensitive perennial grown more for its highly decorative, heart-shaped leaves than for the spikes of small, light blue flowers. The 4-in., scallop-edged leaves come in combinations of red, orange, purple, white, and green.	●	Late spring to late summer	Height: 1–3' Spacing: 8–12"	Tender	Partial to full shade for best leaf color. Moist soil rich in humus. Plants will grow as perennials in zones 10–11. Grow plants from cuttings or start seeds indoors 8–10 weeks before last frost.
	COLLINSIA CHINESE-HOUSES, INNOCENCE *Collinsia heterophylla*	A California native. Lavender blue-and-white, 2-lipped, ¾-in. flowers encircle stem tops, creating a pagoda effect. Pairs of 1- to 2-in., bright green leaves clasp the stems. A velvety fuzz often covers the entire plant, including the flowers.	○ ● ●	Late spring to late summer	Height: 1–2' Spacing: 6"	Hardy	Dappled sun to light shade. Moist, well-drained soil rich in humus. Sow seeds outdoors in fall or early spring where plants are desired. Deadhead withering flowers to prolong blooming season. This is an ideal plant for shady rock gardens.
	CONSOLIDA ANNUAL LARKSPUR, ROCKET LARKSPUR *Consolida ambigua*	An easy-to-grow annual that resembles the perennial larkspur. Dense clusters of ¾-in. flowers form spikes on stems with highly dissected leaves. Flower colors range from white to red, purple, and blue.	○ ● ● ●	Summer	Height: 1–4' Spacing: 6–12"	Hardy	Full sun to partial shade. Fertile, well-drained soil rich in organic matter. Keep soil moist throughout growing season. In warm regions sow seeds outdoors in autumn; elsewhere sow outdoors in early spring.

Annuals for American Gardens

		Flower Color	Time of Bloom	Growth Habit	Hardiness	Growing Conditions
CONVOLVULUS BUSH MORNING-GLORY, DWARF MORNING-GLORY *Convolvulus tricolor*	A morning-glory with a bushy, erect form, ideal for containers or borders. The flashy, 1½-in., funnel-shaped, bicolored flowers usually have bands of blue and white with yellow centers. Rose red cultivars are available.	○ ● ●	Late spring to late summer	Height: 6–12" Spacing: 9–15"	Half-hardy	Full sun. Moist, well-drained soil. Sow seeds outdoors where plants are desired or start indoors 6 weeks before the last frost. To improve germination, gently scrape seeds between sheets of sandpaper and soak them overnight before planting.
CORDYLINE CABBAGE TREE, GRASS PALM, GIANT DRACAENA *Cordyline australis*	An evergreen perennial that can become a small tree in the tropics. In temperate areas, it is sometimes grown as an annual for its 1- to 3-ft., sword-shaped leaves that grow in clumps when the plant is young. Mature plants have small white flowers.	○	Late spring to frost	Height: 3–4' Spacing: 10–15"	Half-hardy	Full sun to partial shade. Fertile, well-drained soil rich in humus. Once established cabbage tree is quite drought tolerant.
COREOPSIS CALLIOPSIS, TICKSEED *Coreopsis tinctoria*	One of the most colorful of the coreopsises. This annual has 1¼-in. flowers on wiry stems. Each of the daisylike blossoms has notched, yellow petals with contrasting bands of maroon, dark red, or orange. The leaves are deeply divided.	● ●	Mid-spring to early autumn	Height: 2–3' Spacing: 6"	Hardy	Full sun. Dry, well-drained soil. Sow seeds outdoors where desired in early spring for the first crop, and again in midsummer for autumn flowers. Sow in autumn in warm climates. Plant seeds densely and let the bushy plants thin themselves.
COSMOS COSMOS *Cosmos bipinnatus* YELLOW COSMOS *C. sulphureus*	Longtime favorites for the cutting garden. Erect stems bear threadlike, ferny leaves and bright, 2- to 3-in., daisy-like flowers with broad petals. C. bipinnatus has red, pink, or white flowers; those of C. sulphureus are yellow.	○ ● ●	Late spring to frost	Height: 3–6' Spacing: 1–1½'	Tender	Full sun to very light shade. Well-drained soil. Sow seeds outdoors where plants are desired as soon as possible after the last frost. It takes about 10 weeks for seedlings to produce flowers. Fertilizers tend to reduce flowering.
CREPIS HAWK'S BEARD *Crepis rubra*	An annual that resembles a pink dandelion. The pinkish flower heads, usually darker at their centers, bloom on relatively long stems arising from clumps of lance-shaped, toothed leaves. Like dandelion it produces plumed seeds.	●	Late summer to early autumn	Height: 8–18" Spacing: 6"	Hardy	Full sun. Prefers well-drained, sandy soil, but will grow well in average garden soil. Plant seeds outdoors where plants are desired in fall or early spring.

			Flower Color	Time of Bloom	Growth Habit	Hardiness	Growing Conditions
	CUPHEA CIGAR FLOWER *Cuphea ignea*	A bushy annual with numerous, drooping, 1-in., tubular, bright red flowers. A dark ring surrounds the white opening through which the stamens protrude. The attractive leaves are lance shaped. Cigar flower makes an excellent container plant.	●	Summer	Height: 8–15" Spacing: 1–1½'	Tender	Full sun to partial shade. Well-drained, evenly moist soil rich in humus. Plants can be grown as perennials in zone 10 and warmer or as tender annuals elsewhere. Start seeds indoors 6 weeks before the last frost.
	CYNOGLOSSUM CHINESE FORGET-ME-NOT *Cynoglossum amabile*	A biennial that blooms the first year from seed. Plants bear showy clusters of 5-lobed, elegant, light blue flowers with either white or blue centers. Cultivars are available with white or pink flowers.	○ ◐ ◐	Summer to frost	Height: 1½–2' Spacing: 9–12"	Hardy	Full sun to light shade. Well-drained soil of low or average fertility. Plants produce best flowers without added fertilizers. Sow seeds outdoors in early spring as soon as soil can be easily worked.
	DAHLIA DAHLIA *Dahlia* cultivars	Members of the aster family, available in a wide range of flower sizes and forms and in colors from yellow to orange to red, lavender, and purple. These cultivars are largely hybrids of D. coccinea and D. pinnata.	○ ◐ ◐ ● ●	Summer	Height: 1–10' Spacing: 1½–3'	Tender	Full sun. Well-drained, evenly moist soil that is never completely dry. Start seeds indoors 6–8 weeks before last frost. In autumn dig roots and store in a cool, dry location over winter. Plant tubers 6 in. deep.
	DATURA DOWNY THORN APPLE *Datura metel*	Bushy plant with large (6- to 7-in.), erect, white, trumpet-shaped flowers formed by 5 fused lobes. Outsides of flowers are often tinged light lavender. Broad leaves have shallow, angular lobes. Plant is poisonous.	○ ◐	Summer	Height: 2–5' Spacing: 1½–2'	Tender	Full sun. Humus-rich soil kept relatively moist. Start seeds of this frost-sensitive perennial indoors in late winter or outdoors in zones 10–11. Whiteflies can be a problem with this plant.
	DIANTHUS CHINA PINK *Dianthus chinensis*	An excellent plant for containers, borders, or rock gardens because of its compact form and abundant 1- to 2-in., 5-petaled flowers. Brightly colored flowers are borne singly or in small clusters. Plants may be grown as annuals, biennials, or short-lived perennials.	○ ◐ ●	Early summer to early autumn	Height: 1–1½' Spacing: 8–15"	Hardy	Full sun. Well-drained soil of average fertility. For first year flowers start indoors in mid-winter to early spring and transplant in mid-spring.

Annuals for American Gardens

		Flower Color	Time of Bloom	Growth Habit	Hardiness	Growing Conditions
DIMOR-PHOTHECA CAPE MARIGOLD *Dimorphotheca pluvialis*	A daisylike marigold usually with white outer petals and yellow and purple centers. The 1½- to 2-in. flowers also may be orange or salmon pink and have chalky blue petal backs. The 2- to 3-in. leaves are oval and hairy.	○◑●	Early to late summer	Height: 8–16" Spacing: 6–9"	Tender	Full sun. Well-drained soil kept on the dry side. In wet soils Cape marigold is prone to rot. Plants grow best in warm weather. Sow seeds outdoors in mid-spring where plants are desired.
DOLICHOS HYACINTH BEAN *Dolichos lablab*	Semiwoody vines that bear striking, pointed, purplish leaflets and attractive, ¾- to 1-in., pink, purple, or white pealike flowers. These in turn produce showy, flat, 1- to 3-in., bright magenta or purple pods. These beautiful fruits are edible.	○◑●	Summer	Height: 10–20' Spacing: 2–3'	Half-hardy	Full sun. Average soil conditions. This tender perennial (in zones 10–11) is easy to grow as an annual. After frost plant outdoors in small groups, or start indoors 4–6 weeks before the last frost. Provide support such as fencing.
DOROTHEAN-THUS LIVINGSTONE DAISY *Dorotheanthus bellidiformis*	Branched, prostrate stems with thick oval leaves. Daisylike flowers of rose pink, pale pink, red, orange, or white. Also known as Mesembryanthemum crystallinum.	○◑●●	Late spring to early autumn	Height: 4–8" Spacing: 6–8"	Tender	Full sun. Sandy, dry, well-drained soil. Start indoors in early spring: plant seeds in a sandy medium 10–12 weeks before last frost. In zone 10 and warmer plant outdoors in late autumn. This South Africa native has naturalized in parts of California.
DYSSODIA DAHLBERG DAISY, GOLDEN-FLEECE *Dyssodia tenuiloba*	A bushy southwestern native with finely divided, bristle-tipped, aromatic leaves and ½- to 1-in., daisylike flowers with yellow-orange outer petals and yellow centers. This excellent bedding plant is sometimes listed as Thymophylla tenuiloba.	◑●	Summer	Height: 8–12" Spacing: 8–12"	Half-hardy	Full sun. Dry, well-drained soil. For best success, start seeds indoors 6–8 weeks before the last frost and transplant outdoors after danger of frost has passed.
EMILIA FLORA'S-PAINTBRUSH, TASSEL FLOWER *Emilia javanica*	An annual with bright yellow or red, ½-in., single or double, daisylike flower heads. Most of the long, narrow, gray-green foliage grows low on the stems. This excellent cut flower makes a good addition to dried-flower arrangements.	◑●	Summer	Height: 1–2' Spacing: 6–12"	Tender	Full sun. Well-drained soil; does not tolerate soggy conditions. Tassel flowers are excellent for dry, sandy, or coastal areas. Plant seeds when danger of frost has passed.

			Flower Color	Time of Bloom	Growth Habit	Hardiness	Growing Conditions
	ESCHSCHOLZIA CALIFORNIA POPPY *Eschscholzia californica*	A short-lived perennial that can be grown as an annual just about anywhere. The 1- to 3-in., poppylike flowers project above ferny, gray-green leaves. The bright golden orange, 4-petaled, cupped flowers have golden centers.	●	Spring to autumn	Height: 6–18" Spacing: 6–8"	Hardy	Full sun to partial shade. Well-drained, sandy loam with low fertility. Sow seeds outdoors in fall or early spring where plants are desired. Plants frequently self-seed and can become weedy. Grow this as a perennial in zones 9–10.
	EUPHORBIA SNOW-ON-THE-MOUNTAIN *Euphorbia marginata*	A hardy annual grown mostly for its foliage. The top leaves are white variegated with green, while bottom leaves tend to be uniform light green. White, 1/2-in. flowers with 5 bracts cluster atop erect, branched stems. Milky sap is a skin irritant.	○	Late spring to frost	Height: 1–3' Spacing: 6–12"	Very Hardy	Full sun. Well-drained soil. Plant seeds outdoors in early spring or late fall 1/3 in. deep in the desired location. Wear gloves when working with this plant to avoid contact with sap. Easy to grow and may become invasive.
	EXACUM PERSIAN VIOLET *Exacum affine*	A biennial grown as a tender annual. Abundant, pale lavender blue, 5-petaled, 1/2-in., fragrant flowers with golden anthers cover bushy mounds of small, oval, glossy, evergreen leaves. Persian violet makes an excellent container plant.	● ●	Summer to early autumn	Height: 8–16" Spacing: 8–16"	Tender	Dappled to moderate shade. Moist, well-drained soil. Seeds need light to germinate; to sow sprinkle them on the soil surface and keep moist. Start indoors 8 weeks before the last frost and set out after frost danger has passed.
	FELICIA BLUE MARGUERITE *Felicia amelloides*	A small, evergreen, frost-sensitive annual shrub. This elegant plant bears 1-in., sky blue, yellow-centered, daisy-like flowers on 12-in. stems.	●	Late spring to autumn	Height: 6–18" Spacing: 6–12"	Tender	Full sun. Well-drained soil. Plants won't tolerate wet sites. Grow as a perennial in zones 10–11, as an annual elsewhere. Start seeds indoors 10–12 weeks before last frost and set out after last frost. Plants can also be propagated by cuttings.
	FENNEL *Foeniculum vulgare*	A culinary herb with erect, branched stems covered by many finely divided, feathery leaves. Seeds, stems, and leaves are used in cooking for their anise flavor. Plants bear flattened, 3- to 4-in. clusters of small (1/4-in.), yellow to light green flowers.	●	Summer	Height: 3–6' Spacing: 1–11/2'	Very Hardy	Full sun. Not choosy about soil conditions. Fennel grows most vigorously in warm weather. Sow seeds outdoors in late autumn, late winter, or early spring where plants are desired.

Annuals for American Gardens

		Flower Color	Time of Bloom	Growth Habit	Hardiness	Growing Conditions
GAILLARDIA BLANKET FLOWER *Gaillardia pulchella*	A garden favorite for its daisylike 2- to 3-in. flower heads. Outer petals typically have yellow tips and dark red bases on the outer petals; centers are reddish purple. Cultivars include plants with rounded double heads, dwarf forms, or varied colors.	● ●	Mid-spring to late summer	Height: 1–1½' Spacing: 6–12"	Hardy	Full sun. Dry to average soil. In zone 8 and warmer sow seeds outdoors in winter; elsewhere sow outdoors in early spring. Seeds also may be started indoors 6 weeks before last frost. Blanket flowers grow quickly.
GAZANIA GAZANIA *Gazania linearis* TREASURE FLOWER *G. rigens*	A flowering annual available in either trailing or clumping form. Plants bear large (1½- to 3-in.), daisylike flowers with yellow, gold, brown, or orange petals; the outer petals often have a dark blotch at their bases. Leaves are woolly underneath.	● ● ●	Late spring through summer	Height: 6–16" Spacing: 8–10"	Half-hardy	Full sun. Dry, well-drained soil of relatively low fertility. Do not add fertilizer; it promotes more foliage and fewer flowers. Start indoors 6–8 weeks before the last frost and set out after danger of frost has passed. Plants are drought tolerant.
GERBERA TRANSVAAL DAISY *Gerbera jamesonii*	Striking 3- to 4-in., orange to vermilion, daisylike flowers with golden centers atop stout, leafless stems. White, yellow, and pastel forms are also available. The 8-in., spatula-shaped leaves form a basal rosette.	○ ● ○ ● ●	Summer to winter	Height: 1–1⅔' Spacing: 1–1½'	Half-hardy	Full sun to partial shade; needs afternoon shade in zone 6 and warmer. Well-drained, evenly moist soil. Seeds need light to germinate; sprinkle on the soil surface and keep moist. Start indoors in midwinter.
GILIA QUEEN-ANNE'S-THIMBLE *Gilia capitata*	A native of the Pacific Coast. Plants bear dense, globular, 1½-in. clusters of ½-in., light blue or white, funnel-shaped flowers. The deeply dissected leaves are feathery. *Gilia* makes an excellent cut flower.	○ ●	Summer	Height: 1½–3' Spacing: 9–15"	Hardy	Full sun. Dry, well-drained, sandy-loam or even gravelly soil. In zone 9 and warmer sow seeds outdoors in autumn; sow outdoors in early spring elsewhere.
GLAUCIUM HORNED POPPY, SEA POPPY *Glaucium corniculatum* *G. flavum*	Poppylike, 2- to 3-in. flowers on erect stems with few leaves. *G. corniculatum is* shorter and has orange to red flowers with dark spots. *G. flavum has* yellow flowers and golden stamens. Both have blue-green basal leaves.	● ●	Summer to early autumn	Height: 1½–3' Spacing: 1–1½'	Hardy	Full sun. Well-drained soil. In zone 9 and warmer sow seeds outdoors in autumn; sow outdoors in early spring elsewhere.

			Flower Color	Time of Bloom	Growth Habit	Hardiness	Growing Conditions
	GOMPHRENA GLOBE AMARANTH *Gomphrena globosa*	A tender annual whose flower heads resemble red clover. The 1-in., globular heads are composed of magenta, pink, white, or even orange chaffy bracts. Leaves have fuzzy hairs on their edges. Gomphrena *is a good dried flower.*	○ ● ● ●	Summer	Height: 8–20" Spacing: 10–15"	Tender	*Full sun. Average, well-drained soil. Plants grow best in warm weather. Start indoors 6–8 weeks before the last frost and set out after danger of frost has passed. For dried flowers, cut stems before flower heads elongate from their globular shape.*
	GOURD YELLOW-FLOWERED GOURD *Cucurbita pepo* var. *ovifera*	A variety of the same species that gives us pumpkins and summer squash. Golden yellow flowers produce hard-shelled, egg-shaped fruits that are often striped in shades of green and yellow. Many different cultivars are available.		Summer	Height: 5–10' Spacing: 9–12"	Tender	*Full sun. Sandy, well-drained soil that is not too fertile. After the last frost, plant seeds in hills where they are to grow. Gourds do not transplant well. To avoid diseases, plant in a different site the next year.*
	GYPSOPHILA ANNUAL BABY'S-BREATH *Gypsophila elegans*	A sprawling, much-branched annual covered with numerous, $1/4$- to $3/4$-in. white flowers with 5 notched petals. Tiny leaves occur in pairs. Cultivars are available with larger flowers and in shades of pink.	○ ●	Mid-spring to early autumn	Height: $1^1/2$–2' Spacing: 1–$1^1/3$'	Hardy	*Full sun, with afternoon shade in zone 9 and warmer. Soil of dry to average moisture, preferably with additional lime. Plant where desired in early spring and at monthly intervals thereafter for successive blooms.*
	HELIANTHUS SUNFLOWER *Helianthus annuus*	Magnificent North American native grown for its large (6- to 12-in.) flower heads and edible seeds. Usually a ring of yellow outer petals surrounds a dark center, but cultivars include forms with white, orange, and deep red flowers.	○ ● ●	Early summer to frost	Height: 5–10' Spacing: 15–20"	Hardy	*Full sun to very light shade. Well-drained, average to dry soil. In early spring, plant the seeds $1/2$ in. deep in the desired location. An aggressive plant, sunflower needs plenty of room.*
	HELICHRYSUM STRAWFLOWER *Helichrysum bracteatum*	One of the most popular species for dried-flower arrangements. The 1- to $2^1/2$-in., white, red, orange, or yellow flower heads grow on erect, branching stems. Lance-shaped leaves are coarsely toothed.	○ ● ●	Summer to early autumn	Height: $1^1/4$–$2^1/2$' Spacing: 9–15"	Half-hardy	*Full sun. Well-drained soil kept on the dry side. Easy to grow. Sow seeds outdoors after last frost, or start indoors 4–6 weeks before last frost and transplant outdoors after danger of frost has passed.*

Annuals for American Gardens

		Flower Color	Time of Bloom	Growth Habit	Hardiness	Growing Conditions
HELIOTROPIUM HELIOTROPE *Heliotropium arborescens*	A shrubby, tender perennial grown as an annual. Dense, flat clusters of small (¹/₂-in.), lavender to white flowers have the fragrance of vanilla. Deep green leaves are small and wrinkled. Plants bloom into winter in zone 10.	○ ●	*Summer*	Height: 1–3' Spacing: 1–1¹/₄'	Tender	*Full sun; afternoon shade in zones 9–11. Humus-rich, well-drained soil. Plants grow best in warm weather. Start indoors 10–12 weeks before last frost; set out after frost danger has passed. Pinch back to make plant bushy.*
HELIPTERUM SWAN RIVER EVERLASTING *Helipterum manglesii* *H. roseum*	A popular everlasting that bears 1- to 2-in., white, rose, red, or pink flower heads with contrasting centers. Flowers close at night. The woolly leaves are 4-in., elongated ovals in H. manglesii, but shorter and narrower in H. roseum.	○ ● ●	*Summer to early autumn*	Height: 9–15" Spacing: 6–8"	Tender	*Full sun. Average to dry, well-drained sandy-loam soil. Start indoors 6–8 weeks before the last frost and carefully set out the fragile seedlings when all danger of frost has passed.*
HUMULUS JAPANESE HOPS *Humulus japonicus*	A flowering vine that climbs by twining its stems around objects. Attractive, coarsely toothed, rough leaves have 5–7 deep lobes and long stems. The insignificant green flowers grow in dangling clusters and produce papery, conelike fruits.	●	*Summer to frost*	Height: 10–20' Spacing: 1–1¹/₂'	Hardy	*Full sun. Well-drained soil rich in humus. Plant seeds where desired in mid-spring and provide support. Plants may self-sow or become weedy in subsequent years.*
HUNNE-MANNIA MEXICAN TULIP POPPY *Hunnemannia fumariifolia*	A frost-sensitive perennial grown as an annual. The chalice-shaped, 2- to 3-in., satiny flowers resemble yellow California poppies with many golden stamens at their centers. The deeply cut leaves are gray green.	●	*Early summer to frost*	Height: 1–2' Spacing: 6–8"	Half-hardy	*Full sun. Well-drained soil with dry to average moisture conditions. In zone 9 and warmer sow seeds outdoors in late autumn. Elsewhere sow outdoors in early spring.*
HYPOESTES POLKA-DOT PLANT *Hypoestes phyllostachya*	A frost-sensitive perennial grown as a foliage plant, often in containers. Pointed, oval, 2- to 3-in., dark green leaves are polka-dotted with splotches of pink. Lavender flowers appear in the leaf axils, but are seen only when grown as a houseplant.	●	*Summer*	Height: 1–2¹/₂' Spacing: 1–2'	Tender	*Full sun to light shade. Well-drained, moist, humus-rich soil. Plants respond to periodic additions of fertilizer. Propagate by cuttings or start seeds indoors 8–10 weeks before last frost; set out after frost danger has passed. Pinch tips to make bushy.*

	Flower Color	Time of Bloom	Growth Habit	Hardiness	Growing Conditions
IBERIS ROCKET CANDYTUFT *Iberis amara* GLOBE CANDYTUFT *I. umbellata*	Popular edging or border annuals with dense clusters of 4-petaled, $1/2$-in., white, pink, red, violet, or bicolored flowers. Leaves are lance shaped and dark green. Later-blooming I. amara *has smaller, more fragrant flowers than* I. umbellata.	○ ◐ ◐ ●	Mid-spring to early autumn or very early spring in warm climates	Height: 6–12" Spacing: 5–8"	Hardy	Full sun. Well-drained soil. Plant seeds outdoors in the desired location in fall or early spring. Candytuft grows vigorously and continues to flower nearly until frost.
IMPATIENS IMPATIENS *Impatiens hybrids*	A tender annual used as a bedding plant for its showy mounds of 1- to 2-in., soft-petaled flowers. Colors of single- or double-flowered hybrids range from white to pink, peach, yellow, or even dark red. Bicolored forms are also available.	○ ◔ ◕ ●	Late spring to frost	Height: 6–18" Spacing: 6–12"	Tender	Filtered sun to partial shade. Fertile, well-drained soil with ample moisture. Start seeds indoors 10–12 weeks before the last frost and set young plants outside after danger of frost has passed.
IPOMOEA MOONFLOWER *Ipomoea alba*	A climbing vine with heart-shaped leaves, somewhat prickly stems, and milky sap. Plants bear 5-lobed, cup-shaped, white morning-glory flowers. But unlike other morning-glories, this species has sweet-scented flowers that open in the evening.	○	Summer	Height: 6–10' Spacing: 1–1$1/2$'	Tender	Full sun. Average to moist soil not too rich in organic matter. Soak seeds overnight before planting. Sow seeds where plants are desired after all danger of frost has passed.
IPOMOEA CARDINAL CLIMBER *Ipomoea × multifida*	A climbing morning-glory with broad (4- to 5-in.), feathery leaves cut into 7–15 segments. The bright scarlet, 2-in., 5-sided, trumpet-shaped flowers have white centers.	○ ●	Summer	Height: 6–10' Spacing: 1–1$1/2$'	Tender	Full sun. Average to moist soil not too rich in organic matter. Soak seeds overnight before planting. Sow seeds where plants are desired after all danger of frost has passed.
IPOMOEA CYPRESS VINE *Ipomoea quamoclit*	A tender annual vine with slender, 1$1/2$-in., tubular flowers in orange or scarlet. The oval leaves are cut into narrow, threadlike segments.	● ●	Summer to early autumn	Height: 10–15' Spacing: 1$1/2$–2'	Tender	Full sun. Average to moist soil not too rich in organic matter. Soak seeds overnight before planting. Sow seeds where plants are desired after all danger of frost has passed.

Annuals for American Gardens

		Flower Color	Time of Bloom	Growth Habit	Hardiness	Growing Conditions
IPOMOEA MORNING-GLORY *Ipomoea tricolor*	The classic morning-glory, a tender perennial vine grown as an annual. The 4- to 5-in. flowers are deep blue at the margins and gradually turn white then yellow at their centers. This climber has heart-shaped leaves up to 10 in. wide.	○ ●	Summer	Height: 6–10' Spacing: 1–1½'	Tender	Full sun. Average to moist soil not too rich in organic matter. Soak seeds overnight before planting. Sow seeds where plants are desired after all danger of frost has passed.
IRESINE BEEFSTEAK PLANT, BLOODLEAF *Iresine herbstii*	A frost-sensitive perennial grown as an annual for its foliage rather than for its small flowers. The bright red stems bear pairs of 5-in. leaves that are variegated around the veins in combinations of white, green, red, purple, brown, or yellow.		Late spring to early autumn	Height: 1–2' Spacing: 1–1½'	Tender	Full sun in moist, loamy, well-drained soil. Propagate plants by cuttings in autumn for winter container plants, or in midwinter for planting outside after the last frost.
KOCHIA RED SUMMER CYPRESS *Kochia scoparia* forma *tricophylla*	An annual shrub that grows in a barrel shape. The pale green, narrow, 2-in., hairy leaves turn violet magenta in autumn. Flowers are inconspicuous. Red summer cypress makes an excellent temporary hedge, but can cause hay fever.		Summer to frost	Height: 2–4' Spacing: 1½–2'	Half-hardy	Full sun. Average to dry, well-drained soil. Start in peat pots 2 months before last frost and plant outdoors after the last frost. Peat pots are necessary because plants can be difficult to transplant. Do not cover seeds; they need light for germination.
LAGURUS HARE'S-TAIL GRASS *Lagurus ovatus*	An ornamental annual grass with soft, creamy white, fuzzy seed heads up to 1½ in. long. Narrow leaves are covered with soft hairs. Seed heads serve as excellent additions to dried-flower arrangements.	○	Summer	Height: 1–1⅔' Spacing: 2–4"	Hardy	Full sun. Average, well-drained soil. Start indoors in small peat pots 8 weeks before the last frost; plant several seeds in each pot. Transplant in groups of several pots, with the groups spaced 4 in. apart.
LANTANA WEEPING LANTANA *Lantana montevidensis*	Vinelike or weeping perennial shrubs grown as annuals with 1½-in. clusters of small, tubular, rose-lilac flowers. Pairs of 1-in. leaves have crinkled surfaces and small teeth. Can be used as a pot plant or ground cover. Fruits and leaves are poisonous.	● ●	Summer, or all year in warm climates	Height: 2–4' Spacing: 1–1½'	Half-hardy	Full sun. Average soil. This perennial blooms through the winter in zone 9 and warmer. In zone 8 and colder, start indoors from cuttings or seeds in late winter and transplant after the last frost.

		Flower Color	Time of Bloom	Growth Habit	Hardiness	Growing Conditions
LATHYRUS SWEET PEA *Lathyrus odoratus*	A favorite old-fashioned vine with clusters of fragrant, 1- to 2-in. flowers in white, pink, red, or purple. Fruits are 2-in. hairy pods. Cultivars are available in bush and dwarf forms.	○ ◖ ◖ ● ●	Late spring to midsummer or winter in warm climates	Height: 4–6' Spacing: 6–15"	Hardy	Full sun. Moist, well-drained, slightly alkaline soil enriched with lime if necessary. Plant seeds 2 in. deep outdoors where plants are desired in late autumn or early spring. Provide supports or plant along stone walls. Deadhead to prolong bloom.
LAVATERA TREE MALLOW *Lavatera trimestris*	A bushy, branching plant that bears numerous, solitary, 4-in., hollyhock-like flowers with 5 broad petals. Cultivars offer flowers in pink, red, or white. Both stems and oval, lobed leaves are hairy.	○ ◖ ●	Summer to early autumn	Height: 2–3' Spacing: 1½–2'	Hardy	Full sun. Well-drained soil not too rich in humus. Tree mallow grows best in cool weather. Plant seeds outdoors where desired 4–6 weeks before last frost. Leaf rust, a disease, sometimes is a problem.
LAYIA TIDY-TIPS *Layia platyglossa*	A California grasslands native named for the white tips on the yellow ray petals that encircle its golden flower centers. The stems and coarsely toothed, elongated leaves are covered with dense hairs.		Spring to early summer	Height: 4–16" Spacing: 4–6"	Tender	Full sun. Well-drained soil that is moist at least in early spring. In zone 9 and warmer sow seeds outdoors in desired location in late fall to early spring. Elsewhere start seeds indoors 6–8 weeks before the last frost.
LIMNANTHES MEADOW FOAM *Limnanthes douglasii*	A sprawling Pacific Coast native. Frothy, feathery, highly dissected leaves cover the ground beneath cupped, 1-in. flowers on long stalks. The fragrant, bicolored flowers have 5 notched petals with white tips and gold bases.	○	Late spring to midsummer	Height: 4–12" Spacing: 4"	Hardy	Full sun. Well-drained soil kept relatively moist. Grows best in cool weather. In zone 9 and warmer sow seeds outdoors where plants are desired in autumn; sow outdoors in early spring elsewhere. A good choice for rock gardens and meadows.
LIMONIUM STATICE *Limonium sinuatum*	A biennial grown as an annual and a superb cutting flower, either fresh or dried. The 5-petaled, 3/8-in. flowers are borne in showy, branched clusters. The classic cultivar is bicolored blue and white, but lavender, rose, and yellow cultivars are also available.	○ ◔ ◔ ● ●	Late summer to frost	Height: 1–2½' Spacing: 1–1¼'	Half-hardy	Full sun. Well-drained soil kept on the dry side. Start seeds indoors in peat pots 8–10 weeks before last frost; transplant after danger of frost has passed.

Annuals for American Gardens

		Flower Color	Time of Bloom	Growth Habit	Hardiness	Growing Conditions
LINARIA TOADFLAX *Linaria maroccana*	An annual graced with spikes of small (1/2-in.) flowers resembling bicolored snap-dragons. The flower's yellow-spotted lower lip projects backward into a spur. The light green leaves are lance shaped. Toadflax is an excellent cut flower.	● ●	Late spring to late summer	Height: 8–16" Spacing: 6"	Very Hardy	Full sun to light shade. Average to moist, well-drained soil. Toadflax grows well in warm weather if sufficient moisture is provided. Sow seeds outdoors in early spring where plants are desired.
LINUM FLOWERING FLAX *Linum grandiflorum*	An excellent rock garden plant. Thin stems with small, blue-green, somewhat clasping leaves set off clusters of brilliant red or pink, 5-petaled, 1- to 1½-in. flowers. Each flower lasts only one day, but there are many in each cluster.	● ●	Late spring to late summer	Height: 1–2' Spacing: 2–3"	Hardy	Full sun. Sow seeds directly where plants are desired. In zone 9 and warmer sow in late autumn; elsewhere sow in early spring. Do not thin; plants grow best in dense stands.
LOBELIA EDGING LOBELIA *Lobelia erinus*	A favorite for edging and window boxes. This annual forms sprawling mounds of bright blue, 2-lipped flowers nestled in dainty, linear foliage. Often flowers have contrasting white or yellow centers. Cultivars available with red or white flowers.	○ ● ●	Late spring to late summer	Height: 3–8" Spacing: 8–10"	Half-hardy	Full sun to partial shade; needs afternoon shade in zone 8 and warmer. Average to moist, well-drained soil. Lobelia grows best in cool weather. Start seeds indoors 10–12 weeks before last frost. To prolong bloom, cut back lightly in midsummer.
LOBULARIA SWEET ALYSSUM *Lobularia maritima*	An easy-to-grow, frost-sensitive perennial usually grown as an annual. Sweet alyssum forms low, dense mounds of petite, 4-petaled white, lavender, pink, or violet flowers. The masses of flowers obscure the small green leaves.	○ ● ● ●	Late spring to frost, or all year in warm climates	Height: 3–12" Spacing: 6–12"	Hardy	Full sun to light shade. Well-drained, moist garden soil. Plant can be grown as a winter annual (or perennial) in warm regions. Sow seeds outdoors in early spring where plants are desired. Prune after first wave of flowering to prolong bloom.
MALCOLMIA VIRGINIA STOCK *Malcolmia maritima*	A fragrant favorite characterized by prolific terminal clusters of 4-petaled, 1-in. flowers in magenta, red, creamy white, or lavender. With branching stems and a compact form, Malcolmia is good for rock gardens and walls or massed in a border.	○ ● ●	Late spring to late summer	Height: 6–12" Spacing: 3–5"	Hardy	Full sun. Rich, well-drained soil. Scatter seeds outdoors on the surface of the soil where plants are desired. In zone 9 and warmer sow seeds in autumn; sow in early spring elsewhere. Successive sowings extend the flowering season.

		Flower Color	Time of Bloom	Growth Habit	Hardiness	Growing Conditions
MATTHIOLA STOCK *Matthiola incana*	A biennial that can be grown as an annual. The dense clusters of white, yellow, red, pink, or blue flowers are fragrant. Usually there are 4 petals, but many cultivars have double flowers. Leaves are dusty gray green.	◯ ◔ ◔ ●	Late spring to early autumn or late winter in warm climates	Height: 1–2½' Spacing: 3–6"	Hardy	Full sun. Average soil kept on the dry side. Thickly sow seeds outdoors in the very early spring where plants are desired. In zone 9 and warmer sow outdoors in late summer to early winter. Do not thin the plants.
MATTHIOLA EVENING STOCK *Matthiola longipetala*	A sprawling stock with very fragrant, dull purple, ¾-in. flowers that open in the evening. Flowers have narrower petals than those of common stock. Cultivars are available with bright purple, yellow, or pink flowers.	◔ ●	Summer	Height: 1–1½' Spacing: 3–6"	Hardy	Full sun to partial shade. Average garden soil. Thickly sow seeds outdoors in very early spring where plants are desired. In zone 9 and warmer sow outdoors in late summer to early winter. Do not thin. Plants self-sow and can become weedy.
MENTZELIA BLAZING STAR *Mentzelia lindleyi*	A California native whose 5-petaled stars open in the evening with a shower of golden stamens at their centers. The groups of 2 or 3 fragrant, 2-in. flowers usually close by early afternoon. The toothed, dandelion-like leaves are hairy.		Spring	Height: 1–4' Spacing: 5–7"	Half-hardy	Full sun. Average, well-drained soil. Sow seeds outdoors ⅛ in. deep in autumn in zone 9 and warmer, or in mid-spring elsewhere. Soil should be evenly moist as seedlings are growing, but on the dry side as flowers begin to appear.
MIMULUS MONKEY FLOWER *Mimulus × hybridus*	A frost-sensitive perennial grown as an annual for its bold, puffy, 2-in., double-lipped flowers with 2 lobes on the upper lip and 3 on the lower. Cultivars come in deep red, yellow, or a patterned combination. Leaves attach to stems in pairs.	●	Early summer to mid-autumn	Height: 12–14" Spacing: 5–7"	Tender	Partial to full shade. Moist, well-drained soil rich in humus. Monkey flower grows best in cool weather. Sow seeds indoors 10–12 weeks before the last frost. Plants make excellent container plants in winter.
MIRABILIS FOUR-O'CLOCK *Mirabilis jalapa*	A sturdy perennial bush grown as an annual and covered with 2-in., trumpet-shaped flowers in red, pink, white, or yellow, or with stripes. The fragrant flowers open in late afternoon, giving the plant its common name. Many cultivars are available.	◯ ◔ ●	Summer	Height: 1½–3' Spacing: 1–2'	Tender	Full sun. Average soil. Start indoors in peat pots 10–12 weeks before the last frost; transplant after all danger of frost has passed. In zones 9–11 sow seeds outdoors where plants are desired in late autumn.

Annuals for American Gardens

		Flower Color	Time of Bloom	Growth Habit	Hardiness	Growing Conditions
MOLUCCELLA BELLS-OF-IRELAND *Moluccella laevis*	An easy-to-grow annual whose common name refers to the small (½-in. or less) white, 2-lipped flowers set in large, green, cuplike calyxes, like clappers in a bell. The green bells grow in whorls that completely cover the tops of 3-ft. stems.	○	Summer	Height: 2–3' Spacing: 9–12"	Hardy	Full sun. Moist, well-drained soil. Seeds need light to germinate; sow outdoors on the soil surface in early spring where plants are desired. Bells-of-Ireland makes an excellent cut flower, either fresh or dried.
MYOSOTIS FORGET-ME-NOT *Myosotis sylvatica*	A sturdy, bushy annual or biennial with loose clusters of clear blue, ⅓-in. flowers with contrasting centers of yellow or white. The leaves have fine, sticky hairs. Many cultivars are available with white, pink, or all-blue flowers.	○ ● ●	Late winter to early summer	Height: 8–24" Spacing: 6–12"	Hardy	Full sun to shade. Moist, well-drained soil. Forget-me-not grows best in cool weather. Sow seeds outdoors in the early spring in zone 7 and colder or in late autumn elsewhere.
NEMESIA NEMESIA *Nemesia strumosa*	A bushy annual with pouched, spurred, irregular, 5-lobed flowers in bright colors or combinations borne in clusters atop branches. Pairs of bright green, toothed leaves become smaller toward the top of the plant.	○ ● ● ● ●	Late spring to early autumn	Height: 1–2' Spacing: 5–6"	Tender	Full sun to partial shade. Well-drained, moist soil. Start seeds indoors 4–6 weeks before the last frost. Nemesia grows best where the growing season is long and cool, as in the Pacific Northwest.
NEMOPHILA BABY-BLUE-EYES *Nemophila menziesii*	A West Coast native. The common name refers to the 1- to 1½-in., 5-petaled flowers with blue tips, white centers, and bright blue stripes or flecks. The 5 stamens have dark blue anthers. The pairs of ferny, divided leaves are hairy.	○ ● ●	Late spring to summer or winter to early spring in warm climates	Height: 10–20" Spacing: 5–10"	Hardy	Full sun to partial shade. Well-drained soil kept moist but not wet. Length of the flowering season depends on moisture. In zone 9 and warmer plant seeds outdoors in late autumn; elsewhere plant in early spring.
NICANDRA APPLE-OF-PERU *Nicandra physalodes*	A rapidly growing annual related to the tomato. Its common name comes from its 2-in., spherical green fruits. The 5-lobed, 1- to 2-in., bell-shaped flowers are violet blue with white throats. The oval leaves are toothed.	○ ●	Summer to early autumn	Height: 2–3' Spacing: 1–1½'	Half-hardy	Full sun. Well-drained, preferably sandy-loam soil. In zone 9 and warmer sow seeds outdoors during early spring. Elsewhere start seeds indoors in a sandy medium in late winter and transplant 2–3 weeks before last frost. May be weedy in zone 10.

			Flower Color	Time of Bloom	Growth Habit	Hardiness	Growing Conditions

NICOTIANA
FLOWERING TOBACCO, JASMINE TOBACCO
Nicotiana alata

A relative of leaf tobacco whose flowers open in late afternoon, releasing perfume all night. The 2- to 4-in., tubular, white, pink, red, or green flowers flare to 1-in., 5-lobed stars. Erect, slender stems and light green, lance-shaped leaves are velvety.

Flower Color: ○ ● ● ●
Time of Bloom: Early summer to early autumn
Growth Habit: Height: 2–5' / Spacing: 8–10"
Hardiness: Half-hardy
Growing Conditions: Full sun to partial shade. Average to moist soil. To sow, lightly dust seeds over soil surface. Sow seeds directly where plants are desired at time of last frost or start indoors 6–8 weeks before last frost. Nicotiana makes a good houseplant.

NICOTIANA
FLOWERING TOBACCO
Nicotiana sylvestris

A frost-sensitive perennial grown as an annual. Fragrant, delicate, night-blooming white flowers have thin, 3- to 5-in. tubes that flare to ½-in., 5-lobed stars at their tips. The rough leaves are often more than 1 ft. long.

Flower Color: ○
Time of Bloom: Late summer to early autumn
Growth Habit: Height: 4–5' / Spacing: 1½–2'
Hardiness: Half-hardy
Growing Conditions: Dappled sun to partial shade. Average to moist soil. To start plants, lightly dust the fine seeds over soil surface, and do not cover. Sow seeds directly where plants are desired at time of last frost. Or start seeds indoors 6–8 weeks before last frost.

NIEREMBERGIA
CUPFLOWER
Nierembergia hippomanica

A mounded, branching perennial grown as an annual. It is covered with white or pale blue, 5-lobed, cupped flowers with yellow centers. Leaves are narrow. Cupflowers are excellent for borders, rock gardens, and hanging baskets.

Flower Color: ○ ●
Time of Bloom: Summer to early autumn
Growth Habit: Height: 6–8" / Spacing: 6–8"
Hardiness: Half-hardy
Growing Conditions: Full sun to light shade. Moist, well-drained soil. Grow as a perennial in zone 9 and warmer; in these zones plant seeds outdoors in late winter. Elsewhere start seeds indoors 10–12 weeks before the last frost.

NIGELLA
LOVE-IN-A-MIST
Nigella damascena

A hardy annual whose common name refers to its lacy leaves and bracts surrounding puffy, often double-petaled, 1½-in., white or pastel flowers. Petals are notched at the tips. Flowers and dried spiny fruits are good for arrangements.

Flower Color: ○ ● ● ●
Time of Bloom: Summer to mid-autumn
Growth Habit: Height: 1–1½' / Spacing: 6–8"
Hardiness: Very Hardy
Growing Conditions: Full sun. Average to moist, well-drained soil. Nigella is easy to grow. In zone 8 or warmer sow seeds in winter where plants are desired; sow in early spring elsewhere. Successive monthly sowings prolong the flowering season.

OMPHALODES
NAVELWORT
Omphalodes linifolia

A delicate annual with narrow, gray-green, lance-shaped leaves and loose, 1-sided spikes of 5-petaled flowers. Each round petal has a vein embossed from its tip to where the bases join. Navelwort is an excellent rock garden plant.

Flower Color: ○
Time of Bloom: Summer to mid-autumn
Growth Habit: Height: 6–12" / Spacing: 4–6"
Hardiness: Hardy
Growing Conditions: Full sun to partial shade. Moist, well-drained soil that is slightly acidic. Do not add any lime; add peat moss to acidify soil if needed. Sow seeds outdoors in early spring where plants are desired.

Annuals for American Gardens

		Flower Color	Time of Bloom	Growth Habit	Hardiness	Growing Conditions
OXYPETALUM SOUTHERN STAR, STAR-OF-THE-ARGENTINE *Oxypetalum caeruleum*	A twining, climbing plant with open clusters of 5-lobed, star-shaped, light blue flowers that darken with age. Stems are covered with soft, fuzzy hairs. Smooth fruits grow to 5–6 in. long.	○	Summer to early autumn	Height: 2–3' Spacing: 8–12"	Tender	Full sun. Average, well-drained soil. Plants can be grown as perennials in zones 10–11; elsewhere grow as annuals. Start seeds indoors 6–8 weeks before last frost and transplant after last frost.
PAPAVER ICELAND POPPY *Papaver nudicaule*	A poppy whose 1- to 3-in. blooms range from red to orange, yellow, and white. Long stems rise above rosettes of deeply cut, hairy leaves. All parts of Iceland poppy are poisonous. A perennial often grown as an annual.	○○●●	Late winter to early autumn	Height: 8–18" Spacing: 6–8"	Hardy	Full sun to partial shade. Average to dry, well-drained soil. Plants grow best in cool weather. In zone 8 and warmer sow seeds outdoors in late autumn for late winter flowers. Elsewhere sow seeds in fall or early spring. Dead-head to prolong bloom.
PAPAVER CORN POPPY, FIELD POPPY, FLANDERS POPPY *Papaver rhoeas*	The traditional, weedy wild-flower of northern Europe. The species has bright red, 2-in., 4-petaled flowers with black centers, but cultivars are available with pink, rose, coral, or white flowers. The stems are tall and branching.	○○●	Late spring to early summer	Height: 1–3' Spacing: 10–12"	Hardy	Full sun. Well-drained, sandy soil. Plants grow best in cool weather. In zone 8 and warmer sow seeds outdoors in late winter. Elsewhere sow seeds outdoors in early spring. Deadhead to pro-long bloom.
PELARGONIUM MARTHA WASHINGTON GERANIUM, MARTHA WASHINGTON PELARGONIUM *Pelargonium × domesticum*	A hybrid geranium bearing among the most ornate blossoms of the common pelargoniums. Flowers are red, white, or pink; the upper 2 petals are blotched with darker colors. The lobed leaves are 2- to 4-in. wide. Many cultivars are available.	○●●	Late spring to early autumn	Height: 1–1½' Spacing: 6–12"	Tender	Full sun to partial shade. Average soil. Plants grow best in areas with cool nights. Propagate from cuttings or start seeds indoors, with bottom heating, 10–12 weeks before last frost. Transplant outdoors after last frost.
PELARGONIUM ZONAL GERANIUM, ZONAL PELARGONIUM *Pelargonium × hortorum*	The most commonly grown pelargonium. The name zonal refers to a dark horse-shoe-shaped zone on each leaf. The many-flowered clusters are often flat-topped and usually red, pink, coral, or white. Many cultivars are available.	○●●	Late spring to early autumn	Height: 1–3' Spacing: 9–15"	Tender	Full sun to partial shade. Average garden soil. Plants grow best with cool nights. Propagate from cuttings or start seeds indoors, giving bottom heating, 10–12 weeks before last frost. Transplant outdoors after last frost.

PELARGONIUM
IVY GERANIUM,
IVY PELARGONIUM
Pelargonium peltatum

A trailing pelargonium with star-shaped, ivylike leaves and clusters of 5–7 flowers, each 2–2½ in. wide. Flowers usually come in red, deep rose, or white, but many cultivars are available. This is a perfect plant for hanging baskets.

Flower Color: ○ ◔ ◕ ●
Time of Bloom: Late spring to early autumn
Growth Habit: Height: 1½–2½' Spacing: 6–12"
Hardiness: Tender
Growing Conditions: Full sun to partial shade. Average soil. Plants grow best in areas with cool nights. Propagate from cuttings or start seeds indoors, with bottom heating, 10–12 weeks before last frost. Transplant outdoors after last frost.

PENNISETUM
FEATHERTOP GRASS
Pennisetum villosum

An ornamental grass with 4-in., cylindrical spikes of flowers forming 1- to 1½-in.-wide feathery plumes atop long stems. The numerous narrow leaf blades grow mostly near the stem base. Feathertop is excellent in dried arrangements.

Flower Color: ○ ◔ ◕
Time of Bloom: Summer to autumn
Growth Habit: Height: 1–2' Spacing: 1–1½'
Hardiness: Half-hardy
Growing Conditions: Full sun. Average soil conditions. Sow seeds outdoors in early spring in zone 7 and warmer; sow outdoors in mid-spring elsewhere. Or start seeds indoors 6 weeks before last frost and plant outdoors when all frost danger is past.

PETUNIA
GARDEN PETUNIA
Petunia × hybrida

A popular old-fashioned annual. The 2- to 4-in., 5-lobed, funnel-shaped flowers come in red, pink, purple, and white; cultivars provide striped, ruffled, fringed, bicolored, single, double, and dwarf forms.

Flower Color: ○ ◕ ● ●
Time of Bloom: Late spring to early autumn
Growth Habit: Height: 8–18" Spacing: 10–12"
Hardiness: Half-hardy
Growing Conditions: Full sun to partial shade. Average to moist, well-drained soil. Start seeds by sowing them on the soil surface in peat pots 8–10 weeks before the last frost. Do not cover seeds as they need light to germinate.

PHACELIA
CALIFORNIA BLUEBELLS
Phacelia campanularia

A creeping native of the Southwest that forms showy carpets with deep blue, 5-lobed, vase-shaped flowers held in loose clusters. The 1-in. leaves are round or heart-shaped and covered with fine hairs that cause a mild rash in some people.

Flower Color: ●
Time of Bloom: Midwinter to early summer
Growth Habit: Height: 6–24" Spacing: 6"
Hardiness: Half-hardy
Growing Conditions: Full sun. Sandy, well-drained soil. Sow seeds outdoors in autumn in zone 9 and warmer; sow outdoors in mid-spring elsewhere. Successive plantings at 4-week intervals will prolong the flowering season.

PHASEOLUS
SCARLET RUNNER BEAN
Phaseolus coccineus

A perennial ornamental bean grown as an annual and bearing showy, brilliant scarlet, 1-in., pealike flowers. The edible young pods and seeds are an additional bonus. The climbing, twining vines have leaves with 3 leaflets.

Flower Color: ●
Time of Bloom: Early to mid-summer
Growth Habit: Height: 6–10' Spacing: 2–4"
Hardiness: Half-hardy
Growing Conditions: Full sun. Moist, well-drained soil rich in humus. Plant seeds outdoors in mid-spring a few weeks after the last frost. Provide tall supports for the vines to grow on.

Annuals for American Gardens

			Flower Color	Time of Bloom	Growth Habit	Hardiness	Growing Conditions
PHLOX ANNUAL PHLOX *Phlox drummondii*	An east Texas native whose trumpet-shaped, 5-lobed flowers, in brilliant pink, red, purple, or white, rise in clusters above hairy stems and leaves. Individual flowers remain open for about a week. Phlox makes an excellent cut flower.		○ ● ● ●	Spring to late summer	Height: 6–18" Spacing: 6–12"	Tender	Full sun. Well-drained soil. Plant seeds outdoors in autumn in zone 8 and warmer; elsewhere sow indoors 8 weeks before last frost. To prolong the flowering season, provide sufficient moisture and deadhead spent blossoms.
PLATYSTEMON CREAMCUPS *Platystemon californicus*	A sturdy California native with a compact form. Solitary, 1-in., creamy yellow, cup-shaped flowers rise on long stems above slender, gray-green leaves. The centers of the 6-petaled flowers have many yellow stamens.		○	Summer	Height: 6–12" Spacing: 4–6"	Hardy	Full sun. Well-drained, moist soil. Plants grow best in cool weather. Sow seeds outdoors where plants are desired in early spring.
PORTULACA PORTULACA, ROSE MOSS *Portulaca grandiflora*	A slow-growing annual ground cover with showy, brightly colored, bowl-shaped flowers in yellow, orange, pink, white, or magenta. Spreading, succulent stems bear fleshy, lance-shaped leaves.		○ ● ● ●	Summer to early autumn	Height: 6–8" Spacing: 6–8"	Tender	Full sun. Average, well-drained soil. For more abundant flowers, do not add fertilizer. Plants are easy to grow. Start seeds indoors in flats 4–6 weeks before last frost; transplant when all danger of frost has passed.
PROBOSCIDEA DEVIL'S CLAW, UNICORN PLANT *Proboscidea louisianica*	A sprawling annual with 3-lobed, broad leaves and tubular, somewhat flattened, mauve-and-white flowers. These produce 6-in., edible pods with a curved beak that splits into 2 parts, giving this southeastern native its common names.		○ ●	Summer to frost	Height: 2–3' Spacing: 6–12"	Tender	Full sun. Average soil conditions. In zone 8 and warmer sow seeds outdoors where plants are desired in mid-spring; elsewhere start indoors 6–8 weeks before the last frost. Plants can become weedy in warm climates.
RESEDA MIGNONETTE *Reseda odorata*	A hardy annual whose clusters of small, creamy white blossoms grow on short stems and make excellent cut flowers. The fragrant, 1/3-in., star-shaped flowers have 4–7 fringed petals and orange stamens. They are attractive to bees.		○	Summer to early autumn or early spring in warm climates	Height: 4–8" Spacing: 6–12"	Very Hardy	Full sun to partial shade. Well-drained soil rich in humus. Plants grow best in cool weather. Sow seeds outdoors where plants are desired in early spring or fall in warm climates. Successive sowings at monthly intervals prolong the flowering season.

		Flower Color	**Time of Bloom**	**Growth Habit**	**Hardiness**	**Growing Conditions**
RICINUS CASTOR BEAN *Ricinus communis*	A robust, fast-growing annual grown more for its large (1- to 3-ft.), tropical leaves, often bronze or variegated in red, than for its peculiar, round, spiny, seedpods. Both the seedpods and the seeds are highly poisonous.	● ● ●	Summer	Height: 3–15' Spacing: 2–3'	Tender	Full sun. Well-drained soil. Plants are easy to grow. In zone 9 and warmer plant seeds outdoors in mid-spring. Elsewhere start seeds indoors 6 weeks before last frost and plant outdoors after danger of frost has passed. Plants may be weedy in warm areas.
RUDBECKIA BLACK-EYED SUSAN *Rudbeckia hirta* GLORIOSA DAISY *R. hirta* 'Gloriosa Daisy'	A native perennial that can be grown as an annual. The 2-in. daisylike flowers have deep yellow outer petals and domed, silky, deep brown centers. The cultivar 'Gloriosa Daisy' is larger and has outer petals banded with dark red.	● ●	Midsummer to early autumn	Height: 1–2' Spacing: 9–15"	Hardy	Full sun to very light shade. Well-drained soil. Sow seeds outdoors in autumn or early spring. Although plants are short-lived, they reseed well and may become weedy in the garden. Rudbeckia is an ideal plant for wildflower meadows.
SALPIGLOSSIS PAINTED-TONGUE *Salpiglossis sinuata*	An erect, fast-growing annual. Showy, 2-in., multicolored flowers surrounded by leafy bracts grow in clusters. The funnel-shaped flowers, with 5 notched lobes, come in combinations of red, gold, pink, blue, and yellow.	● ● ● ●	Summer to early autumn	Height: 2–3' Spacing: 10–12"	Tender	Full sun. Moist, well-drained soil. For abundant flowering, do not add fertilizer. Plants grow best in cool weather. Start seeds indoors by sowing on surface of soil 6–8 weeks before last frost. Seeds require darkness to germinate.
SALVIA MEALY-CUP SAGE *Salvia farinacea* 'Victoria' SCARLET SAGE *S. splendens*	Ornamental sages grown as annual bedding plants for their showy clusters of 2-lipped flowers. S. farinacea 'Victoria' is larger, more branching, and has blue flowers. S. splendens is more compact and has bright scarlet flowers.	● ●	Summer to frost	Height: 1–4' Spacing: 6–12"	Half-hardy	Full sun to partial shade. Well-drained, moist soil. In zone 8 and warmer sow seeds outdoors in mid-spring. Elsewhere start seeds indoors 6–8 weeks before last frost.
SANVITALIA CREEPING ZINNIA *Sanvitalia procumbens*	A low-growing annual whose abundant flowers make it an excellent choice for rock gardens and hanging baskets. Small (1-in.), yellow, daisylike flowers with large, dark centers grow on creeping stems with pairs of pointed, oval leaves.		Summer	Height: 5–6" Spacing: 6–12"	Tender	Full sun. Average to dry, well-drained soil. Creeping zinnias hold up well to heat and high humidity. Sow seeds outdoors where plants are desired in late spring after all danger of frost has passed.

Annuals for American Gardens

		Flower Color	Time of Bloom	Growth Habit	Hardiness	Growing Conditions
SCABIOSA PINCUSHION FLOWER, SWEET SCABIOUS *Scabiosa atropurpurea*	A favorite cut flower with long stems and long-lasting, domed flower heads. The terminal heads are clusters of tiny, tubular flowers, in colors ranging from purple to pink to white, and surrounded by leafy bracts.		Early summer to early autumn	Height: 2–3' Spacing: 8–10"	Half-hardy	Full sun. Average to alkaline soil. Scabiosa responds favorably to additions of lime and is easy to grow. Start seeds indoors 4–6 weeks before the last frost. Set out plants near the last frost date. Plants grow best in cool weather.
SCHIZANTHUS BUTTERFLY FLOWER *Schizanthus × wisetonensis*	Showy clusters of 1½-in. flowers resembling a mass of hovering butterflies. Colors include ornately patterned reds, yellows, blues, pinks, and white. The upper lip of the flower is often streaked with yellow. Foliage is feathery.		Summer to early autumn	Height: 1–2' Spacing: 6–12"	Tender	Full sun to partial shade. Rich, moist, well-drained soil. Plants grow best in areas with cool summers. Sow seeds indoors on the soil surface 12 weeks before last frost. Although seeds should not be covered by soil, they need darkness to germinate.
SETARIA FOXTAIL MILLET *Setaria italica*	An ornamental grass with 4- to 8-in., bristly, cylindrical seed heads on long stems. Plants create a stunning visual effect in late afternoon or early morning light. Rough leaf blades have a pungent odor when crushed.		Late summer to mid-autumn	Height: 3–5' Spacing: 4–6"	Hardy	Full sun. Average soil. This grass is easy to grow. Sow seeds outdoors where plants are desired in early spring. Do not thin. Plants self-sow and may become weedy.
TAGETES MARIGOLD, AFRICAN MARIGOLD *Tagetes erecta* FRENCH MARIGOLD *T. patula*	Familiar garden annuals available in hundreds of cultivars. T. erecta is larger, with uniform yellow or orange, single or double flowers. The smaller T. patula has orange or yellow flowers streaked or blotched with red.		Late spring to frost	Height: 5–30" Spacing: 3–15"	Half-hardy	Full sun. Average soil. Plants are easy to grow. Start seeds indoors 4–6 weeks before the last frost. Set out plants after danger of frost has passed. Pinch back tips to make plants bushier. Deadhead plants to prolong bloom.
THUNBERGIA BLACK-EYED SUSAN VINE *Thunbergia alata*	A fast-growing vine whose yellow to gold, 5-lobed, pouched flowers with dark purple centers bloom in profusion. The 2-in., toothed, heart-shaped leaves are attractive on their own. Plants grow best climbing on a trellis or a fence.		Early summer to early autumn	Height: 5–10' Spacing: 1–1¼'	Tender	Full sun to partial shade. Moist, well-drained soil rich in humus. In zone 9 and warmer plant seeds outdoors in early spring. Elsewhere start indoors 6–8 weeks before all danger of frost has passed.

		Flower Color	Time of Bloom	Growth Habit	Hardiness	Growing Conditions
TITHONIA MEXICAN SUNFLOWER *Tithonia rotundifolia*	A shrubby, frost-sensitive perennial grown as an annual for its 2- to 3-in., daisylike flower heads with orange or scarlet petals encircling golden yellow centers. The large, coarse leaves are somewhat rounded.	● ●	Summer to early autumn	Height: 4–5' Spacing: 2–2½'	Tender	Full sun. Dry, well-drained soil. Plants grow best in hot weather. In zone 9 and colder start seeds indoors 6–8 weeks before the last frost. Elsewhere plant seeds where plants are desired in early spring.
TORENIA BLUEWINGS, WISHBONE FLOWER *Torenia fournieri*	An annual with unusual 5-petaled flowers with dark blue-purple markings at the flaring petal edges. The throat of the flower is light lavender with a yellow blotch on the lowest petal. Fused stamens resemble a wishbone.	● ●	Midsummer to early autumn	Height: 6–12" Spacing: 6–8"	Tender	Partial shade. Well-drained, moist, fertile soil. Start seeds indoors in zone 8 and colder, sowing seeds 10–12 weeks before the last frost. Elsewhere sow seeds outdoors in early spring after soil has warmed.
TRACHYMENE BLUE LACE FLOWER *Trachymene coerulea*	An annual resembling a blue version of Queen-Anne's-lace. The 2- to 3-in., flat-topped or rounded clusters of tiny flowers grow on long stems. Pale green leaves are deeply divided and ferny. Plants make excellent cut flowers.	●	Summer	Height: 1–3' Spacing: 6–10"	Hardy	Full sun. Sandy-loam soil. Densely sow seeds outdoors where plants are desired in the early spring. Do not thin; let these weak-stemmed plants support each other.
TROPAEOLUM NASTURTIUM *Tropaeolum majus*	A popular annual with showy, edible flowers and foliage. 2- to 3-in. flowers, usually yellow or orange, may be spotted or streaked with red. Round leaves attach to stems at their centers. Dwarf and vinelike cultivars are available.	● ●	Early summer to early autumn	Height: 1–12' Spacing: 12–18"	Tender	Full sun to partial shade. Average, well-drained soil. For abundant flowers do not add fertilizer. Plants grow best in cool weather. Sow seeds outdoors where plants are desired after all danger of frost has passed.
TROPAEOLUM CANARY-BIRD FLOWER, CANARY CREEPER *Tropaeolum peregrinum*	A rapidly growing annual vine that makes a good screen. Pale yellow, fringed, irregular, 1-in. flowers with long, green-spurred lower petals bloom on sprawling vines with deeply lobed, bird's-foot foliage.		Summer to frost	Height: 5–8' Spacing: 1–1½'	Tender	Full sun to partial shade. Average to moist, well-drained soil. For abundant flowers do not add fertilizer. Plants grow best in cool weather. Sow seeds outdoors where plants are desired after all danger of frost has passed.

Annuals for American Gardens

		Flower Color	Time of Bloom	Growth Habit	Hardiness	Growing Conditions
VERBENA GARDEN VERBENA *Verbena × hybrida*	Low-growing, frost-sensitive perennials with toothed, spatula-shaped leaves and fragrant, 5-petaled flowers in compact clusters. The notched petals range in color from white to yellow, red, pink, or purple. Many cultivars are available.		Summer	Height: 1–1½' Spacing: 6–8"	Tender	Full sun to partial shade; needs some shade in zone 9 and warmer. Well-drained soil rich in humus. Plants grow best in warm weather. Start seeds indoors 10–12 weeks before the last frost. Set out plants after danger of frost has passed.
VINCA PERIWINKLE *Vinca major* 'Variegata'	A frost-sensitive perennial often used as an annual ground cover or container plant. Trailing vines have pairs of glossy green, oval leaves variegated in light yellow. Vinca has light blue or white flowers that are most abundant in spring.		Late spring to early summer	Height: 4–8" Spacing: 6–12"	Half-hardy	Full sun to full shade. Moist, well-drained soil. Propagate from cuttings placed in a constantly moist, but not wet, sandy medium in late winter.
VIOLA PANSY *Viola × wittrockiana*	A familiar garden favorite, with 2- to 5-in., 5-petaled flowers bearing facelike markings. The bottom petal has a spur with sweet nectar. Numerous cultivars come in a wide variety of single colors and combinations.		Late spring to winter	Height: 5–9" Spacing: 6–8"	Very Hardy	Full sun to partial shade. Moist, well-drained soil rich in humus. Start seeds indoors 2 months before last frost and then transplant outside about a month before last frost. Deadhead to prolong flowering. Some varieties bloom into winter.
XERANTHEMUM IMMORTELLE *Xeranthemum annuum*	A hardy annual with ever-lasting flowers in white, purple, magenta, or pink. The true flowers in the center of the flower head are surrounded by papery bracts of the same color. Gray-green, elongated leaves grow mostly near the bases of the stems.		Summer to early autumn	Height: 1½–2' Spacing: 6–9"	Hardy	Full sun. Average to moist, well-drained soil. In zone 5 and colder start seeds in peat pots 8 weeks before last frost. Elsewhere sow out-doors where plants are desired in early spring. Do not thin.
ZINNIA ZINNIA *Zinnia elegans*	An extremely popular annual whose flower heads come in every color but blue. Plant size varies from compact miniatures with small flowers to giants with flower heads exceeding 4 in. Cactus-flowered varieties have twisted petals.		Summer to early autumn	Height: 4–36" Spacing: 4–18"	Tender	Full sun to very light shade. Average to dry, well-drained soil. Sow seeds outdoors where desired after the last frost, or start indoors 4–6 weeks before the last frost. Transplant after frost danger has passed. Young plants will not tolerate frost exposure.

Annuals Listed by Hardiness

The categories of hardy, half-hardy, and tender annuals are fully described on page 6–9. Hardy annuals can tolerate the most cold; many will grow as winter flowers in zones 9–11. Half-hardy annuals can tolerate a bit of light frost, and grow best in cool weather. Tender annuals must have warm conditions to grow.

Hardy Annuals

Annual baby's-breath (*Gypsophila elegans*), annual larkspur (*Consolida ambigua*), baby-blue-eyes (*Nemophila menziesii*), bachelor's-button (*Centaurea cyanus*), bells-of-Ireland (*Moluccella laevis*), black-eyed Susan (*Rudbeckia hirta*), blanket flower (*Gaillardia pulchella*), blue lace flower (*Trachymene coerulea*), borage (*Borago officinalis*), California poppy (*Eschscholzia californica*), calliopsis (*Coreopsis tinctoria*), Canterbury-bells (*Campanula medium*), China pink (*Dianthus chinensis*), Chinese forget-me-not (*Cynoglossum amabile*), Chinese-houses (*Collinsia heterophylla*), creamcups (*Platystemon californicus*), Cupid's-dart (*Catananche caerulea*), dusty-miller (*Centaurea cineraria*), evening stock (*Matthiola longi-petala*), farewell-to-spring (*Clarkia amoena*), fennel (*Foeni-culum vulgare*), field poppy (*Papaver rhoeas*), flowering flax (*Linum grandiflorum*), forget-me-not (*Myosotis sylvatica*), foxtail millet (*Setaria italica*), globe candytuft (*Iberis umbellata*), gloriosa daisy (*Rudbeckia hirta* 'Gloriosa Daisy'), hare's-tail grass (*Lagurus ovatus*), hawk's beard (*Crepis rubra*), hollyhock (*Alcea rosea*), honeywort (*Cerinthe major*), horned poppy (*Glaucium* spp.), Iceland poppy (*Papaver nudicaule*), immortelle (*Xeranthemum annuum*), Japanese hops (*Humulus japonicus*), love-in-a-mist (*Nigella damascena*), meadow foam (*Limnanthes douglasii*), mignonette (*Reseda odorata*), navelwort (*Omphalodes linifolia*), ornamental kale (*Brassica oleracea* acephala group), pansy (*Viola × wittrockiana*), partridge pea (*Cassia fasciculata*), pot marigold (*Calendula officinalis*), quaking grass (*Briza maxima*), Queen-Anne's-thimble (*Gilia capitata*), red thistle (*Cirsium japonicum*), rocket candytuft (*Iberis amara*), snapdragon (*Antirrhinum majus*), snow-on-the-mountain (*Euphorbia marginata*), stock (*Matthiola incana*), sunflower (*Helianthus annuus*), sweet alyssum (*Lobularia maritima*), sweet pea (*Lathyrus odoratus*), toadflax (*Linaria maroccana*), tree mallow (*Lavatera trimestris*), tricolor chrysanthemum (*Chrysanthemum carinatum*), Virginia stock (*Malcolmia maritima*)

Half-Hardy Annuals

African daisy (*Arctotis stoechadifolia*), African marigold (*Tagetes erecta*), apple-of-Peru (*Nicandra physalodes*), blazing star (*Mentzelia lindleyi*), bush morning-glory, (*Convolvulus tricolor*), cabbage tree (*Cordyline australis*), California bluebells (*Phacelia campanularia*), corn cockle (*Agrostemma githago*), cupflower (*Nierembergia hippomanica*), Dahlberg daisy (*Dyssodia tenuiloba*), edging lobelia (*Lobelia ̈erinus*), feather-top grass (*Pennisetum villosum*), flowering tobacco (*Nicotiana* spp.), French marigold (*Tagetes patula*), hyacinth bean (*Dolichos lablab*), Job's tears (*Coix lacryma-jobi*), mealy-cup sage (*Salvia farinacea* 'Victoria'), Mexican tulip poppy (*Hunnemannia fumariifolia*), musk mallow (*Abelmoschus moschatus*), periwinkle (*Vinca major* 'Variegata'), petunia (*Petunia × hybrida*), pincushion flower (*Scabiosa atropurpurea*), pocketbook plant (*Calceolaria integrifolia*), prickly poppy (*Argemone mexicana*), red summer cypress (*Kochia scoparia* forma *tricophylla*), scarlet runner bean (*Phaseolus coccineus*), scarlet sage (*Salvia splendens*), spider flower (*Cleome hasslerana*), statice (*Limonium sinuatum*), strawflower (*Helichrysum bracteatum*), sweet-sultan (*Centaurea moschata*), Transvaal daisy (*Gerbera jamesonii*), treasure flower (*Gazania rigens*), weeping lantana (*Lantana montevidensis*)

Tender Annuals

Beefsteak plant (*Iresine herbstii*), black-eyed Susan vine (*Thunbergia alata*), blue marguerite (*Felicia amelloides*), blue pimpernel (*Anagallis monelli*), bloodflower (*Asclepias curassavica*), bush violet (*Browallia speciosa*), butterfly flower (*Schizanthus × wisetonensis*), canary creeper (*Tropaeolum peregrinum*), canna (*Canna × generalis*), Cape marigold (*Dimorphotheca pluvialis*), cardinal climber (*Ipomoea × multifida*), castor bean (*Ricinus communis*), China aster (*Callistephus chinensis*), cigar flower (*Cuphea ignea*), cockscomb (*Celosia cristata* Childsii group), coleus (*Coleus × hybridus*), cosmos (*Cosmos* spp.), creeping zinnia (*Sanvitalia procumbens*), cup-and-saucer vine (*Cobaea scandens*), dahlia (*Dahlia* cultivars), downy thorn apple (*Datura metel*), elephant's-ear (*Caladium × hortulanum*), flossflower (*Ageratum houstonianum*), flowering maple (*Abutilon* spp.), four-o'clock (*Mirabilis jalapa*), globe amaranth (*Gomphrena globosa*), gourd (*Cucurbita pepo* var. *ovifera*), heliotrope (*Heliotropium arborescens*), impatiens (*Impatiens* hybrids), ivy geranium (*Pelargonium peltatum*), Joseph's-coat (*Amaranthus tricolor*), Livingstone daisy (*Dorotheanthus bellidiformis*), love-in-a-puff (*Cardiospermum halicacabum*), love-lies-bleeding (*Amaranthus caudatus*), Madagascar periwinkle (*Catharanthus roseus*), Martha Washington geranium (*Pelargonium × domesticum*), Mexican sunflower (*Tithonia rotundifolia*), monkey flower (*Mimulus × hybridus*), moonflower (*Ipomoea alba*), morning-glory (*Ipomoea tricolor*), nasturtium (*Tropaeolum majus*), nemesia (*Nemesia strumosa*), ornamental pepper (*Capsicum annuum*), painted-tongue (*Salpi-glossis sinuata*), Persian violet (*Exacum affine*), plumed cockscomb (*Celosia cristata* Plumosa group), polka-dot plant (*Hypoestes phyllostachya*), rose moss (*Portulaca grandiflora*), star-of-the-Argentine (*Oxypetalum caeruleum*), Swan River daisy (*Brachycome iberidifolia*), Swan River everlasting (*Helipterum* spp.), tassel flower (*Emilia javanica*), tidy-tips (*Layia platyglossa*), unicorn plant (*Proboscidea louisianica*), verbena (*Verbena × hybrida*), wax begonia (*Begonia × semperflorens-cultorum*), winged everlasting (*Ammobium alatum*), wishbone flower (*Torenia fournieri*), zinnia (*Zinnia elegans*), zonal geranium (*Pelargonium × hortorum*)

Resources for Gardening with Annuals

There are many dependable mail-order suppliers that can be helpful for gardeners interested in annuals. A selection is included here. Most have catalogues available upon request (some charge a fee). For further information and supplier suggestions, The Complete Guide to Gardening by Mail is available from the Mailorder Association of Nurseries, Department SCI, 8683 Doves Fly Way, Laurel, MD 20783. Please add $1.00 for postage and handling in the United States ($1.50 for Canada).

Flower Seeds & Plants

Abundant Life Seed
Foundation
P.O. Box 772
Port Townsend,
WA 98368
206-385-7192
Nonprofit foundation selling over 600 varieties of open-pollinated, chemical-free seeds.

W. Atlee Burpee Co.
300 Park Avenue
Warminster, PA 18974
215-674-4900
Seeds and supplies from one of the oldest names in American gardening.

The Cook's Garden
P.O. Box 535
Londonderry, VT 05148
802-824-3400
Herbs, vegetables, flowers, supplies, and books for gardeners.

The Country Garden
Route 2
Crivitz, WI 54114-9645
800-448-2375
A broad seed selection of flowers for cutting gardens.

Henry Field's Seed &
Nursery Co.
415 N. Burnett Street
Shenandoah, IA 51602
605-665-9391
Seeds, supplies, and plants.

Gurney's Seed &
Nursery Co.
110 Capital Street
Yankton, SD 57079
605-665-1930
Seeds, plants, and fertilizers for annuals.

Johnny's Selected Seeds
Foss Hill Road
Albion, ME 04910-9731
207-437-4301
Vegetables, herbs, flowers, supplies, and books for gardeners.

J.W. Jung Seed Co.
335 S. High Street
Randolph, WI 53957
800-247-5864
Broad selection of seeds and nursery stock, also tools and supplies.

Mellinger's Inc.
2310 W. South Range
Road
North Lima, OH 44452
800-321-7444
Seeds, plants, supplies, and tools

Park Seed Co.
Cokesbury Road
Greenwood, SC 29647
803-845-3369
Seeds, plants, bulbs, tools, and a wide selection of gardening supplies.

Pinetree Garden Seeds
Route 100
New Gloucester,
ME 04260
207-926-3400
Seeds, books, and supplies. Specializes in space-saving cultivars.

R. H. Shumway Seeds
P.O. Box 1
571 Whaley Pond Road
Graniteville, SC 29829
800-322-7288
Good variety of annual seeds.

Stokes Seeds, Inc.
Box 548
Buffalo, NY 14240-0548
716-695-6980
Flower and vegetable seeds and supplies for commercial farmers and home gardeners.

Thompson & Morgan
P.O. Box 1308
Jackson, NJ 08527-0308
800-274-7333
Seeds of all types and a wide range of garden supplies.

Herbs & Everlasting Flowers

Comstock, Ferre & Co.
P.O. Box 125
263 Main Street
Wethersfield, CT 06109
800-753-3773
Flower and vegetable seeds, including many everlastings.

DeGiorgi Seed Company
6011 N Street
Omaha, NE 68117-1634
800-858-2580
Broad selection of old-fashioned annuals for cut or dried arrangements.

Nichols Garden Nursery
1190 N. Pacific Highway
Albany, OR 97321-4598
503-928-9280
Extensive selection of seeds for herbs and everlastings as well as books and supplies.

Shepherd's Garden Seeds
6116 Highway 9
Felton, CA 95018
For advice: 408-335-6910
To order: 203-482-3638
Vegetables, herbs, and specialties such as everlastings and edible flowers.

Ornamental Grasses & Wildflowers

Clyde Robin Seed Co.
3670 Enterprise Avenue
Hayward, CA 94545
800-647-6475
Wide range of wildflower seeds.

Prairie Nursery
P.O. Box 306
Westfield, WI 53964
608-296-3679
Prairie plants, seeds, and native grasses.

Richters
357 Highway 47
Goodwood, Ontario
Canada LOC 1AO
416-640-6677
Seeds of many herbs, everlasting flowers, and wildflowers.

Vermont Wildflower Farm
Route 7, Box 5
Charlotte, VT 05445
802-425-3500
Wildflower seeds and seed mixes for sun or shade.

Wildlife Nurseries, Inc.
P.O. Box 2724
Oshkosh, WI 54903
414-231-3780
Suppliers of grasses, aquatic plants, and wetland plants, as well as plants to attract wildlife.

Regional Specialties

High Altitude Gardens
P.O. Box 1048
Hailey, ID 83333
208-788-4363
Seeds selected for their ability to grow at high altitudes.

Ed Hume Seeds, Inc.
P.O. Box 1450
Kent, WA 98035
206-859-1110
Untreated flower, herb, and vegetable seeds for short-season climates.

Kilgore Seed Co.
1400 W. First Street
Sanford, FL 32771
407-323-6630
Seeds carefully selected for their ability to grow in Florida, Gulf Coast states, and other tropical and subtropical areas.

Native Seeds/SEARCH
2509 N. Campbell #325
Tucson, AZ 85719
602-327-9123
Native seeds of the Southwest and Mexico, collected and propagated with long-term preservation in mind and distributed free to Native Americans.

Redwood City Seed Co.
P.O. Box 361
Redwood City, CA 94064
415-325-7333
Old-fashioned varieties, including many unusual imports.

Seeds Blum
Idaho City Stage
Boise, ID 83706
208-342-0858
Vegetables, annuals, and perennials for various conditions.

Supplies & Accessories

Alsto's Handy Helpers
P.O. Box 1267
Galesburg, IL 61401
800-447-0048
Selection of easy-to-use tools and garden products.

Country Home Products
P.O. Box 89
Ferry Road
Charlotte, VT 05445
800-446-8746
Mowers, trimmers, clippers, composters, and various garden tools.

Earth-Rite
Zook & Ranck, Inc.
RD 1, Box 243
Gap, PA 17527
800-332-4171
Fertilizers and soil amendments for lawn and garden.

Garden Way, Inc.
102nd Street & 9th Avenue
Troy, NY 12180
800-833-6990
Mowers, rototillers, garden carts, and other lawn and garden equipment.

Gardener's Eden
P.O. Box 7303
San Francisco, CA 94120
800-822-9600
Many items appropriate for gardeners, including outdoor containers, tools, and accessories.

Gardener's Supply Co.
128 Intervale Rd.
Burlington, VT 05401
800-876-5520
Gardening products, gifts, accessories, greenhouse kits, and composting equipment.

Gardens Alive!
5100 Schenley Place
Lawrenceburg, IN 47025
812-537-8650
Beneficial insects and a complete line of supplies for organic gardening.

Home Gardener
Manufacturing Company
30 Wright Avenue
Lititz, PA 17543
800-880-2345
Composting and related gardening equipment.

Kemp Company
160 Koser Road
Lititz, PA 17543
800-441-5367
Shredders, chippers, and other power equipment.

Plow & Hearth
P.O. Box 830
Orange, VA 22960
800-866-6072
Gardening tools and products as well as garden ornaments and furniture.

Ringer Corporation
9959 Valley View Road
Eden Prairie, MN 55344
612-941-4180
Organic soil amendments, beneficial insects, and garden tools.

Smith & Hawken
2 Arbor Lane
Box 6900
Florence, KY 41022-6900
800-776-3336
Well-crafted tools as well as containers, supplies, and furniture.

Solutions
P.O. Box 6878
Portland, OR 97228
800-342-9988
Home and gardening products designed to make jobs easier.

Index

Photo Credits

All photography credited as follows is copyright © 1994 by the individual photographers. **Karen Bussolini:** pp. 13 (top), 18 (right), 22 (scarlet runner bean), 30, 33 (center), 63 (bottom right); **David Cavagnaro:** pp. 13 (bottom), 15 (bottom), 16 (bottom), 27 (top), 28 (purple cupflower, morning-glory, and petunias), 33 (right), 37 (opium poppies), 59, 77 (bottom right); **Rosalind Creasy:** pp. 20, 21, 22 (canary creeper), 27 (center), 37 (cosmos daisies), 39 (bottom), 58 (calendula, pansies, sweet peas), 70, 83, 84, 85 (bottom), 86; **Ken Druse:** pp. 25 (bottom right), 37 (larkspur); **Derek Fell:** pp. 14 (right), 23, 60, 81, 82; **Dency Kane:** pp. 14 (left), 25 (top), 28 (gerbera daisies), 58 (sweet alyssum, Canterbury-bells), 92; **Peter Loewer:** p. 55; **Tom Moyer:** pp. 25 (bottom left), 28 (French marigolds), 35; **Maggie Oster:** pp. 4, 7, 8, 10, 27 (bottom), 40–41, 50, 78; **Jerry Pavia:** pp. 15 (top), 18 (left), 19 (top, bottom), 22 (angel's trumpet), 31, 37 (snapdragons), 53, 54; **Joanne Pavia:** pp. 34, 56, 85 (top); **Patricia A. Taylor:** p. 38; **Michael S. Thompson:** pp. 22 (hyacinth bean), 24, 26, 28 (nasturtiums, scarlet sage), 32 (left), 57; **Cynthia Woodyard:** pp. 12, 29, 32 (center, right), 33 (left), 37 (Victoria salvia), 39 (top), 64.

Step-by-step photography by Derek Fell.

Front cover photograph copyright © 1994 by Derek Fell.

All plant encyclopedia photography is copyright © 1994 by Derek Fell, except the following, which are copyright © 1994 by the individual photographers. **Rosalind Creasy:** *Ipomoea × multifida;* **Pamela Harper:** *Cardiospermum halicacabum, Cassia fasciculata, Chrysanthemum carinatum, Dorotheanthus bellidiformis, Platystemon californicus;* **Peter Loewer:** *Omphalodes linifolia, Proboscidea louisianica;* **Steven Still:** *Collinsia heterophylla;* **Michael S. Thompson:** *Ammobium alatum, Crepis rubra;* **Cynthia Woodyard:** *Cirsium japonicum.*